Beginning Kotlin

Build Applications with Better Code, Productivity, and Performance

Ted Hagos

Apress®

Beginning Kotlin: Build Applications with Better Code, Productivity, and Performance

Ted Hagos
Makati, Philippines

ISBN-13 (pbk): 978-1-4842-8697-5   ISBN-13 (electronic): 978-1-4842-8698-2
https://doi.org/10.1007/978-1-4842-8698-2

Managing Director, Apress Media LLC: Welmoed Spahr
Acquisitions Editor: Steve Anglin
Development Editor: Laura Berendson
Coordinating Editor: Jill Balzano

Cover designed by eStudioCalamar

Cover image by Akira Hojo on Unsplash (www.unsplash.com)

Distributed to the book trade worldwide by Apress Media, LLC, 1 New York Plaza, New York, NY 10004, U.S.A. Phone 1-800-SPRINGER, fax (201) 348-4505, e-mail orders-ny@springer-sbm.com, or visit www.springeronline.com. Apress Media, LLC is a California LLC and the sole member (owner) is Springer Science + Business Media Finance Inc (SSBM Finance Inc). SSBM Finance Inc is a **Delaware** corporation.

For information on translations, please e-mail booktranslations@springernature.com; for reprint, paperback, or audio rights, please e-mail bookpermissions@springernature.com.

Apress titles may be purchased in bulk for academic, corporate, or promotional use. eBook versions and licenses are also available for most titles. For more information, reference our Print and eBook Bulk Sales web page at http://www.apress.com/bulk-sales.

Any source code or other supplementary material referenced by the author in this book is available to readers on GitHub (https://github.com/Apress). For more detailed information, please visit http://www.apress.com/source-code.

Printed on acid-free paper

For Steph and Adrianne; and also, Wayne, Amy, plus Bagel.

Table of Contents

About the Author

Ted Hagos is the CTO and Data Protection Officer of RenditionDigital International (RDI), a software development company based out of Dublin. Before he joined RDI, he had various software development roles and also spent time as a trainer at IBM Advanced Career Education, Ateneo ITI, and Asia Pacific College. He spent many years in software development dating back to Turbo C, Clipper, dBase IV, and Visual Basic. Eventually, he found Java and spent many years working with it. Nowadays, he's busy with Kotlin, full-stack JavaScript, Android, and Spring applications.

About the Technical Reviewer

Manuel Jordan Elera is an autodidactic developer and researcher who enjoys learning new technologies for his own experiments and creating new integrations. Manuel won the Springy Award 2013 Community Champion and Spring Champion. In his little free time, he reads the Bible and composes music on his guitar. Manuel is known as dr_pompeii. He has tech-reviewed numerous books, including *Pro Spring MVC with WebFlux* (Apress, 2020), *Pro Spring Boot 2* (Apress, 2019), *Rapid Java Persistence and Microservices* (Apress, 2019), *Java Language Features* (Apress, 2018), *Spring Boot 2 Recipes* (Apress, 2018), and *Java APIs, Extensions and Libraries* (Apress, 2018). You can read his detailed tutorials on Spring technologies and contact him through his blog at www.manueljordanelera.blogspot.com. You can follow Manuel on his Twitter account, @dr_pompeii.

Acknowledgments

Thanks to Steve Anglin, Mark Powers, Shonmirin, and Manuel Jordan Elera for making this book possible.

Introduction

Welcome to *Beginning Kotlin*.

Kotlin may have (initially) gained popularity as a drop-in replacement for Java for building Android apps, but it's ubiquitous now. You can use it to build web apps—both on the front and back end. Kotlin is quickly gaining popularity in areas that used to be Java strongholds. If you want to get a head start on Kotlin, this book is an excellent place to start.

Chapter Overviews

Chapter 1 (Introduction to Kotlin) – Brief introduction to the Kotlin language. You'll learn a bit about the language's history and some of its well-known capabilities. The chapter also walks you through the steps on how to install Kotlin and get started with a quick project.

Chapter 2 (A Quick Tour of Kotlin) – Discusses the language elements of Kotlin. You'll learn the syntax with brisk examples. You'll know how to declare strings, variables, and constants. You'll also learn how to move around using Kotlin's control structures for looping, branching, and exception handling.

Chapter 3 (Functions) – There's a whole chapter dedicated to functions because Kotlin's functions have something new up their sleeves. It has all the trimmings of a modern language like default and named parameters, infix functions, and operators, and with Kotlin, we can also create extension functions. Extension functions let you add behavior to an existing class without inheriting from it and without changing its source.

Chapter 4 (Types) – This chapter deals with object-oriented topics. You'll learn how Kotlin treats interfaces, classes, and access modifiers. We'll also learn about the new *data classes* in Kotlin. It also talks about *object declarations*—it's the replacement for Java's *static* keyword.

Chapter 5 (Higher Order Functions and Lambdas) – Now, we go to Kotlins's functional programming capabilities. It discusses how to create and use higher order functions, lambdas, and closures.

Chapter 6 (Collections) – Walks through the classic collection classes of Java and how to use them in Kotlin.

Chapter 7 (Generics) – Using generics in Kotlin isn't that much different from Java. If generics are old hat for you, then most of this chapter will be a review. But try to read through it still because it talks about *reified generics*, which Java doesn't have.

Chapter 8 (Debugging) – Kotlin has plenty of language improvements that help us avoid errors. Still, errors are a big part of a programmer's life. This chapter walks you through the steps to do a debugging session in IntelliJ.

Chapter 9 (Unit Testing) – If you're a fan of unit testing—why shouldn't you be?—this is for you. We'll walk through the steps to write and run unit tests using JUnit5.

Chapter 10 (Writing Idiomatic Kotlin) – Kotlin was designed to be very similar to Java, but it also has plenty of features that make it stand out. This chapter points out those unique Kotlin features and shows examples of how to use them.

Chapter 11 (Creating a Spring Boot Project) – A quick introduction to how to create a Spring Boot project using Kotlin.

Source Code and Supplementary Material

All source code used in this book can be downloaded from github.com/
apress/beginning-kotlin, where you will also find the following online-
only extras:

Appendix A (Java Interoperability) – You can use Kotlin classes
from Java codes and vice versa. This chapter explores Java-Kotlin
interoperability.

Appendix B (Building a Microservices App Part 1) – Spring Boot is
an excellent choice for building microservices. This appendix details how
to build a sample microservices project.

Appendix C (Building a Microservices App Part 2) – Continues from
Appendix B.

Appendix D (Cloud Deployment) – It's the age of cloud-native apps.
This chapter discusses the workflow for bringing Spring Boot apps into
the cloud.

CHAPTER 1

Introduction to Kotlin

Kotlin is a new language that targets the Java platform; its programs run on the JVM (Java Virtual Machine), which puts it in the company of languages like Groovy, Scala, Jython, and Clojure, to name a few.

What we'll cover:

- Overview of the Kotlin language

- How to get Kotlin

- Getting Kotlin running in IntelliJ

Kotlin is from JetBrains, the creators of IntelliJ, PyCharm, WebStorm, ReSharper, and other great development tools. In 2011, JetBrains unveiled Kotlin; the following year, they open-sourced Kotlin under the Apache 2 license. At Google I/O 2017, Google announced first-class support for Kotlin on the Android platform; since then, Kotlin's ubiquity has spread. You can use Kotlin for web development (server-side and/or client-side), desktop development, and of course, mobile development. With Kotlin/ Native in the works (still in beta at the time of writing), you should soon be able to write Kotlin codes that compile to native code that can run without a VM. In this book, we will focus on Kotlin for server-side web development—using Spring Boot.

If you're wondering where the name Kotlin came from, it's the name of an island near St. Petersburg, where most of the Kotlin team is located. According to Andrey Breslav of JetBrains, Kotlin was named after an island just like Java was named after the Indonesian island of Java—however, you

© Ted Hagos 2023
T. Hagos, *Beginning Kotlin*, https://doi.org/10.1007/978-1-4842-8698-2_1

might remember that the history of the Java language contains references that it was named after the coffee, rather than the island.

About Kotlin

It's Simple

```
fun main() {
    val name = "stranger"      // Declare your first variable
    println("Hi, $name!")      // ...and use it!
    print("Current count:")
    for (i in 0..10) {         // Loop over a range
                                  from 0 to 10

        print(" $i")
    }
}
```

As you can see from the preceding code—which I lifted from https:// kotlinlang.org—we don't (always) have to write a class. Top-level functions can run without wrapping them inside classes.

It's Asynchronous

```
import kotlinx.coroutines.*

suspend fun main() {                                        // #1
    val start = System.currentTimeMillis()
    coroutineScope {                                        // #2
        for (i in 1..10) {
            launch {                                        // #3
                delay(3000L - i * 300)                      // #4
                log(start, "Countdown: $i")
```

```
        }
      }
    }
                                                    // #5

    log(start, "Liftoff!")
}

fun log(start: Long, msg: String) {
    println("$msg " +
            "(on ${Thread.currentThread().name}) " +
            "after ${(System.currentTimeMillis() -
            start)/1000F}s")
}
```

#1 This is a function that can be suspended and resumed later.

#2 This statement creates a scope for starting coroutines.

#3 Start ten concurrent tasks.

#4 Pause the execution.

#5 Execution continues when all coroutines in the scope have finished.

It's Object-Oriented

```
abstract class Person(val name: String) {
    abstract fun greet()
}

interface FoodConsumer {
    fun eat()
    fun pay(amount: Int) = println("Delicious! Here's $amount
    bucks!")
}
```

```kotlin
class RestaurantCustomer(name: String, val dish: String) :
Person(name), FoodConsumer {
    fun order() = println("$dish, please!")
    override fun eat() = println("*Eats $dish*")
    override fun greet() = println("It's me, $name.")
}

fun main() {
    val sam = RestaurantCustomer("Sam", "Mixed salad")
    sam.greet() // An implementation of an abstract function
    sam.order() // A member function
    sam.eat() // An implementation of an interface function
    sam.pay(10) // A default implementation in an interface
}
```

Like Java, it's object-oriented. So, all those long hours you've invested in Java's OOP and design pattern won't go to waste. Kotlin classes, interfaces, and generics look and behave quite a lot like Java's. This is definitely a strength because, unlike other JVM languages like Scala, Kotlin doesn't look too foreign. It doesn't alienate Java programmers. Instead, it allows them to build on their strengths.

It's Functional

Kotlin is a functional language. Higher order functions are functions that operate on other functions, either by taking them in as parameters or by returning them.

In a functional language (like Kotlin), functions are not just a named collection of statements. You can use them anywhere you might use a variable. You can pass functions as an argument to other functions, and you can even return functions from other functions. This way, coding allows for a different way of abstraction. Functions are treated as first-class citizens.

```kotlin
fun main() {
    // Who sent the most messages?
    val frequentSender = messages
        .groupBy(Message::sender)
        .maxByOrNull { (_, messages) -> messages.size }
        ?.key                                                // #1
    println(frequentSender) // [Ma]

    // Who are the senders?
    val senders = messages
        .asSequence()                                        // #2
        .filter { it.body.isNotBlank() && !it.isRead }       // #3
        .map(Message::sender)                                // #4
        .distinct()
        .sorted()
        .toList()                                            // #5
    println(senders) // [Adam, Ma]
}

data class Message(                                          // #6
    val sender: String,
    val body: String,
    val isRead: Boolean = false                             // #7
)

val messages = listOf(                                       // #8
    Message("Ma", "Hey! Where are you?"),
    Message("Adam", "Everything going according to plan
    today?"),
    Message("Ma", "Please reply. I've lost you!"),
)
```

#1 Get their names.

#2 Make operations lazy (for a long call chain).

#3 Use lambdas ...

#4 ... or member references.

#5 Convert sequence back to a list to get a result.

#6 Create a data class.

#7 Provide a default.

#8 Create a list.

Ideal for Tests

```
// Tests
// The following example works for JVM only
import org.junit.Test
import kotlin.test.*

class SampleTest {
    @Test
    fun `test sum`() {                          // #1
        val a = 1
        val b = 41
        assertEquals(42, sum(a, b), "Wrong result for
        sum($a, $b)")
    }

    @Test
    fun `test computation`() {
        assertTrue("Computation failed") {
            setup()                             // #2
            compute()
        }
    }
}
```

```
// Sources
fun sum(a: Int, b: Int) = a + b
fun setup() {}
fun compute() = true
```

#1 Write test names with whitespaces in backticks

#2 Use lambda returning the test subject

Other things we can say about Kotlin are the following:

- **It's less ceremonious than Java**. We don't need to explicitly write getters and setters for data objects; there are language features in Kotlin which allow us to do away with such boiler-plate codes. Also, the natural way of writing codes in Kotlin prevents us from ever assigning *null* to a variable. If you want to explicitly allow a value to be *null*, you have to do so in a deliberate way.

- **It's statically and strongly typed**. Another area that Kotlin shares with Java are the type system. It also uses static and strong typing. However, unlike in Java, you don't always have to declare the type of the variable before you use it. Kotlin uses *type inference*.

- **Interoperability with Java**. Kotlin can use Java libraries, and you can use it from Java programs as well. This lowers the barrier to entry in Kotlin, and the interoperability with Java makes the decision to start a new project using Kotlin a less daunting enterprise.

All the sample codes above are from kotlinlang.org. If you'd like to try the codes without investing time (yet) on IDE setup, go to `https://kotlinlang.org`. You should see the code samples I used above (Figure 1-1).

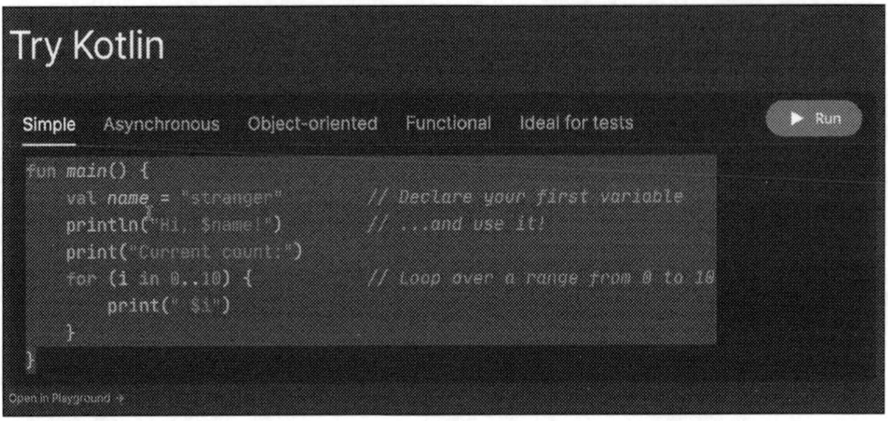

Figure 1-1. *Try Kotlin*

If you click the "Run" button or the "Open in Playground" link, you should be able to run the codes, see the result, and even edit the codes.

The Kotlin playground is good for short snippets and for experimenting. If you intend to do non-trivial coding work in Kotlin, you'll need an IDE.

It is possible to use Kotlin without IntelliJ. You should be able to find Kotlin plugins for Eclipse or NetBeans—you can even use the Kotlin command line SDK if you feel really up to it, but the simplest way to get started is to just use JetBrain's IntelliJ. After all, Kotlin was a brainchild of JetBrains.

Setup and Configuration of IntelliJ

With IntelliJ, you don't need to download the JDK (Java Development Kit) separately; you also don't need to install the Kotlin plugin manually. You can manage both the JDK and Kotlin plugins within IntelliJ.

To download IntelliJ, go to https://jetbrains.com, click "Developer Tools", then "IntelliJ IDEA", as shown in Figure 1-2.

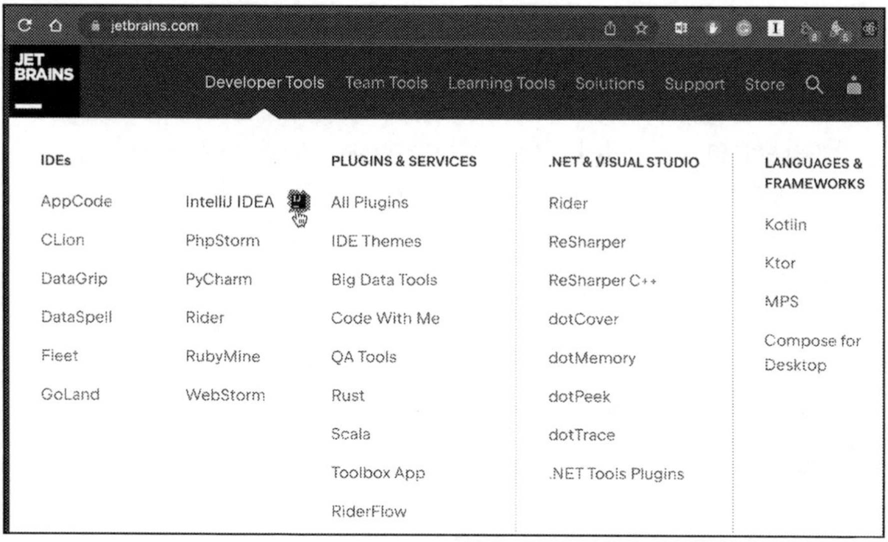
jetbrains.com
JET BRAINS
Developer Tools
Team Tools
Learning Tools
Solutions
Support
Store
IDEs
AppCode
CLion
DataGrip
DataSpell
Fleet
GoLand
IntelliJ IDEA
PhpStorm
PyCharm
Rider
RubyMine
WebStorm
PLUGINS & SERVICES
All Plugins
IDE Themes
Big Data Tools
Code With Me
QA Tools
Rust
Scala
Toolbox App
RiderFlow
.NET & VISUAL STUDIO
Rider
ReSharper
ReSharper C++
dotCover
dotMemory
dotPeek
dotTrace
.NET Tools Plugins
LANGUAGES & FRAMEWORKS
Kotlin
Ktor
MPS
Compose for Desktop

Figure 1-2. *Developer Tools section on the JetBrains site*

Then, in the screen that follows (Figure 1-3), choose either the Community or the Ultimate edition.

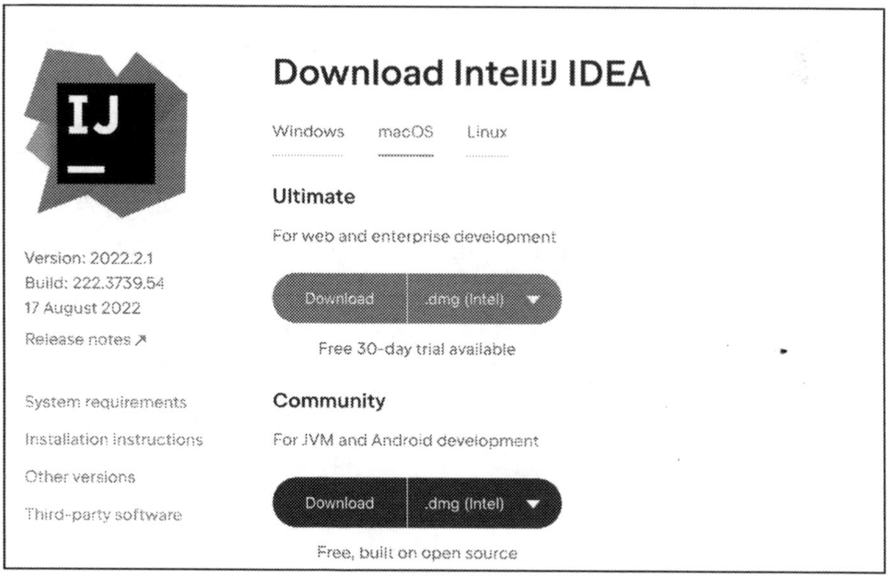
IJ
Download IntelliJ IDEA
Windows
macOS
Linux
Ultimate
For web and enterprise development
Download
.dmg (Intel)
Free 30-day trial available
Version: 2022.2.1
Build: 222.3739.54
17 August 2022
Release notes ↗
System requirements
Installation instructions
Other versions
Third-party software
Community
For JVM and Android development
Download
.dmg (Intel)
Free, built on open source

Figure 1-3. *Download IntelliJ*

You can get the IDEA installer for Windows, macOS, or Linux platforms. There are two editions of IDEA: the Ultimate and Community edition. The Community edition is free for use—it's not a disabled or time-restricted version. It's full-featured, and you can use it as long as you want. The Ultimate edition is the paid version. The difference between the two versions lies in the number of languages, framework support, build tools, and other toolchains—as you may have guessed, the Ultimate edition has all the bells and whistles. For our purposes, the Community edition will do. JetBrains has a detailed comparison between Ultimate and Community editions here `https://www.jetbrains.com/products/compare/?product =idea&product=idea-ce`.

Hardware Requirements

The recommended hardware specs from JetBrains are as follows:

- 8GB RAM

- Multi-Core CPU

- SSD Drive with at least 5GB of free space

- Full HD resolution monitor (1920x1080)

- 64-bit OS

IntelliJ doesn't need a Java runtime (installed beforehand) to install. The IntelliJ installer is bundled with a JRE 11 runtime. Of course, when we build apps, we'll need to download a JDK eventually—but we'll manage from within the IDE already.

On Windows

1. Download the installer from the JetBrains site.

2. Run the installer (double-click) the way you would run any other Windows app.

3. On the installation options, you can configure the following:

   a. Create a desktop shortcut for IDEA.

   b. Add the directory with the IDEA command-line launchers to the Windows PATH environment variable. If you choose this, you can launch IDEA via the command line from any directory.

   c. Add the Open Folder as Project action to the system context menu (right-click action).

   d. Associate some file extensions (Java, Groovy, and Kotlin) extensions with IDEA. If you choose this, IntelliJ will launch whenever you double-click on *.java, .groovy, .kt, or .kts* files. (Figure 1-4 shows the IntelliJ installation options.)

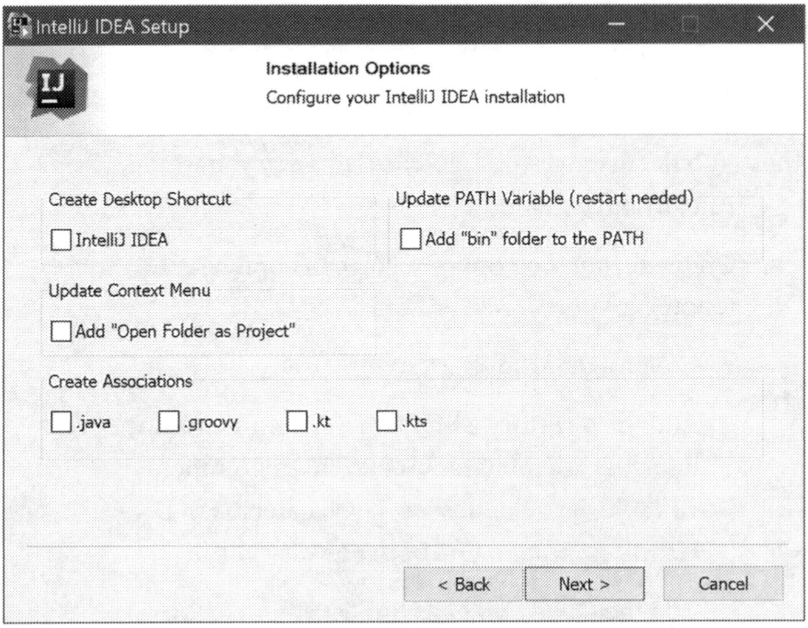

Figure 1-4. *IntelliJ installation options*

You can launch IntelliJ from the Windows Start menu. I usually just hit the Super key (the one with the Windows logo), then type "IntelliJ", then hit Enter. If you created a desktop shortcut, you could double-click that—it'll launch IntelliJ just as well.

On macOS

1. Download the disk image; take care that you're downloading the correct installer for your architecture. There are separate disk images for Intel and Apple Silicon processors.

2. Mount the image and drag the IntelliJ IDEA app to the Applications folder.

There are a couple of ways to launch IDEA:

- Open the Applications folder, then double-click

- Click the Launchpad, find IntelliJ, then click

- Hit spotlight (keyboard shortcut is cmd + ENTER), type "IntelliJ", hit Enter

On Linux

1. Download the tarball

2. Extract the tarball to a directory where you have *rwx* permissions. This can be any subfolder within your /home/yourUsername directory. You can also extract the installer in the /opt folder (which is recommended)

If you want to extract it in the /opt folder, you can run the following command

```
sudo tar -xzf ideaIC.tar.gz -C /opt
```

To launch IntelliJ, execute the **idea.sh** script from the extracted directory.

When you run IntelliJ for the first time, you can take several steps to complete the installation and customize your IDE. There's typically a welcome screen (Figure 1-5).

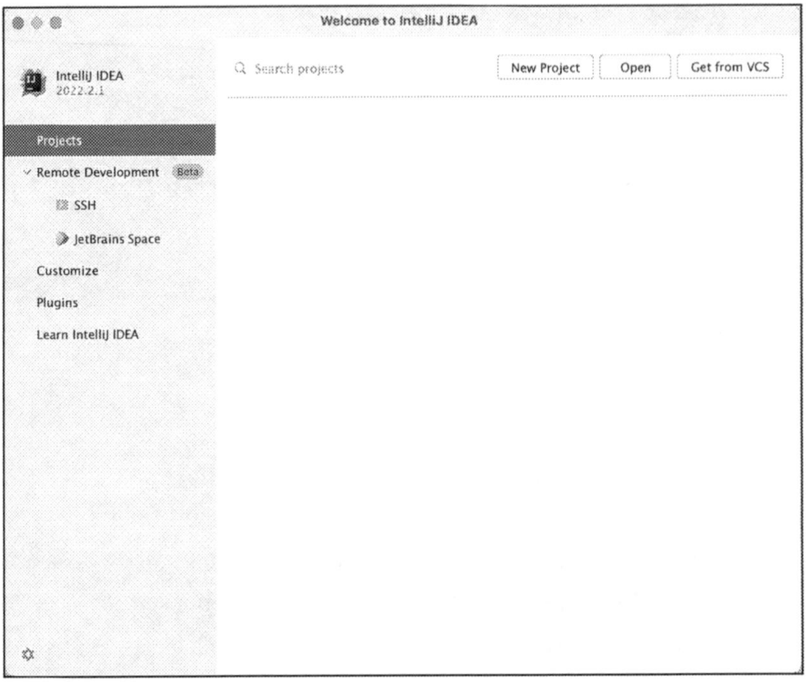

Figure 1-5. *Welcome to IntelliJ IDEA*

The Welcome screen is the starting point for working with the IDE. You can also configure your settings from this screen. This screen also appears when you close all opened projects.

IntelliJ is very configurable. You can tweak many features to suit your preferences.

Getting a Project Up and Running

Launch IDEA if it's not opened yet.

From the Welcome screen, click "New Project". Then, choose "Kotlin Multiplatform", and in the *Project template,* choose "Console Application" (see Figure 1-6).

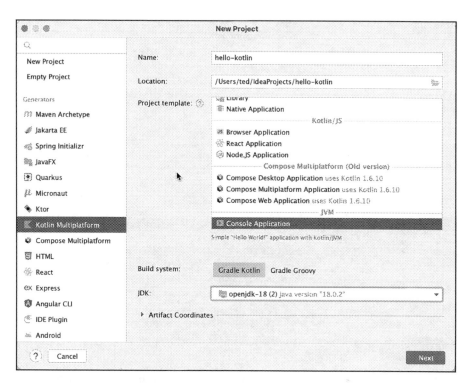

Figure 1-6. *New Project*

Choose "Gradle Kotlin" for the *Build System*. For the JDK, click the down arrow, and choose "Download JDK". Figure 1-7 shows all the JDK in my system; as you can see, I already have a couple of them installed. Kotlin requires JDK 8 to run—feel free to choose between JDK 8 to 18.

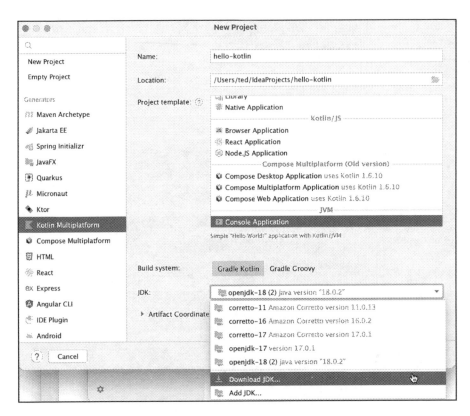

Figure 1-7. *New Project ➤ Download JDK*

Click *Next* to proceed.

Choose the target JVM. I chose 16 because, at the time of writing, Gradle was complaining about 18 (or 17). Leave Junit 5 as the test framework.

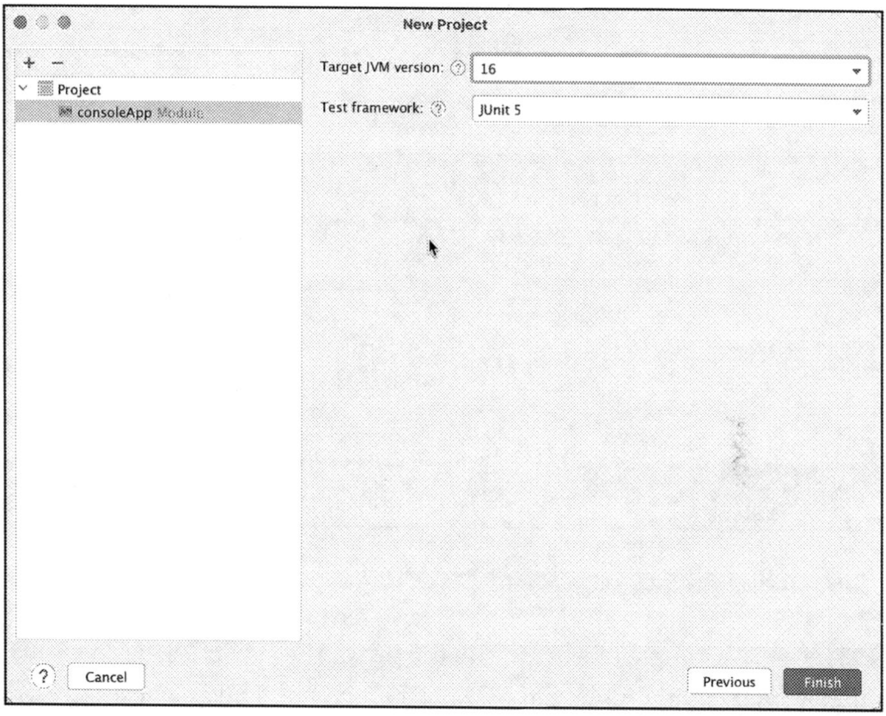

Figure 1-8. *New Project ➤ Target JVM and Test Framework*

Click Finish to proceed.

It will take IntelliJ a while to build the project and index the files, but when it's done, it will open the generated Kotlin file in the main editing panel. See Figure 1-9.

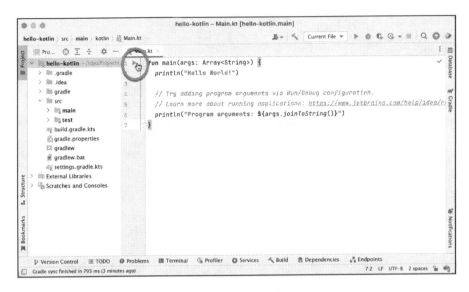

Figure 1-9. *hello-kotlin project* ➤ *Main.kt*

There are a couple of ways to run the project. You can trigger the Run action from the main menu bar or quick launch bar. The quickest way to run is to click the arrow inside the main editor gutter (I marked it in Figure 1-9).

Another way to quickly run the project is to use IntelliJ's search everywhere tool—the Double Shift. Pressing the Shift key twice in quick succession launches the *Search Everywhere,* then type "Run" (see Figure 1-10).

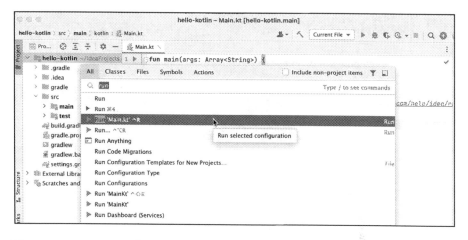

Figure 1-10. *Search Everywhere ➤ Run Main.kt*

Choose the "Run Main.kt" action, then hit Enter. The *Search Everywhere* tool is probably the single most important keyboard shortcut you need to remember in IntelliJ. It can get you anywhere.

Run the app any way you choose. IntelliJ will build the app, then run it. The runtime results show up in the *Run* tool window (lower part of the IDE). See Figure 1-11.

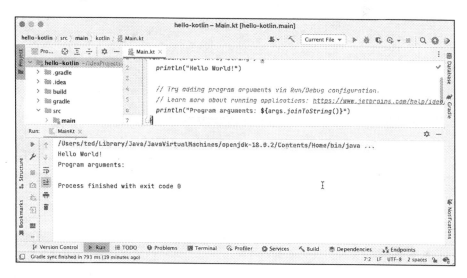

Figure 1-11. *Main.kt runtime result*

Key Takeaways

- Kotlin may have started as a drop-in replacement for Java for Android development, but it's ubiquitous now. You can use it for web development (both front-end and back-end), desktop apps, and, very soon, for writing native apps.

- The easiest way to set up a Kotlin environment is to get IntelliJ (from JetBrains). You don't need the Ultimate edition. The Community edition will suffice.

- There are many things to like about Kotlin; it's simple, functional, asynchronous, object-oriented, and interoperable with Java (among other things).

CHAPTER 2

A Quick Tour of Kotlin

Kotlin is not very different from Java. Kotlin introduced some new language features, but I'm sure you'll find that Kotlin and Java are more similar than they are different. This is good news if you're a Java programmer because it means the learning curve for Kotlin is not steep.

What we'll cover:

- Program elements
- Basic types
- Immutability
- Strings
- Nullable types
- Control structures
- Exception handling

Program Elements

When learning a new language like French or Spanish, you'll probably start with parts of speech and the rules that govern them. It'd be easier to approach a language if we understood how its parts come together.

A Kotlin program contains literals, variables, expressions, keywords, and many other things. We'll explore some of them in this section.

© Ted Hagos 2023

T. Hagos, *Beginning Kotlin*, https://doi.org/10.1007/978-1-4842-8698-2_2

Literals

Kotlin has literal for the basic types (numbers, characters, Boolean, String). *Type* refers to the kind of data that Kotlin recognizes. Listing 2-1 shows a code snippet that defines various types.

Listing 2-1. Literal examples

```
var intLiteral = 5
var doubleLiteral = .02
var stringLiteral = "Hello"
var charLiteral = '1'
var boolLiteral = true
```

In the preceding listing, the values *5, .02, "Hello", '1,'* and *true* are literals of Integer, Double, String, Character, and Boolean types, respectively. By the way, you probably noticed by now that you don't need to terminate Kotlin statements with a semi-colon—you can still do that if you want to. I just chose not to do it.

Variables

We use a variable to store and manipulate data, or more precisely, a value. Values are things that you can store, manipulate, print, push, or pull from an I/O. To work with values, we put them inside variables. You can create a variable by declaring an identifier using the *var* keyword followed by the type, like in the following statement:

```
var foo: Int
```

In the statement above, foo is the identifier and Int is the type. Kotlin specifies types by placing them to the right of the identifier and is separated from it by a colon symbol.

Once you declare a variable, you can assign a value to it, like this

```
foo = 10
```

and then use it in a function, like in the following:

```
println(foo)
```

Like in Java, we can declare and define variables on the same line. Here's the *var foo* example again

```
var foo: Int = 10
println(foo)
```

We can still shorten the assignment statement above by omitting the type (Int). See the sample code below:

```
var foo = 10
println(foo)
```

We don't always have to declare or write the type of the variables. Kotlin is smart enough to figure out the type when you assign a literal value to a variable; it's called *type inference*. On the occasions when we explicitly tell Kotlin the variable's type, notice that it is on the right side of the variable name (foo); while in Java, it's the other way around; the variable type is on the left side of the identifier. Kotlin did not follow the Java convention of putting the type to the left of the identifier, in Kotlin, we don't always have to write the *type*

```
var foo = 10  // compiler knows 10 is an integer literal
var boo = .02 // double literal makes boo a double type
```

Kotlin uses another keyword to declare variables, the *val* keyword. Variables declared with this keyword can be initialized only once within the execution block where they were defined. That makes them effectively constants. While variables created using the var keyword are mutable, you can change them as often as you want. Think of *val* as the equivalent of the *final* keyword in Java; once you initialize it to a value, you can't change it anymore; they're *immutable.*

Val variables are declared and initialized just like *var* variables (see the example below)

```
val a = 10  // declaration and initialization on the same line
```

They can also be declared and initialized later, like the statements below:

```
val a: Int
a = 10
```

Remember that variables declared with the *val* keyword are final and cannot be re-assigned once you've initialized them to a value. The code snippet below will not work

```
val boo = "Hello"
boo = "World" // boo already has a value
```

If you think you need to change the value of the variable boo at a later time, change the declaration from *val* to *var*.

Expressions and Statements

An expression combines operators, functions, literal values, variables, or constants and always resolves to a value. It also can be part of a more complex expression. A statement can contain expressions, but in itself, a statement doesn't resolve to a value. It cannot be part of other statements. A statement is always a top-level element in its enclosing block.

Mostly, what you learned in Java about expressions and statements holds in Kotlin, but there are slight differences. As we go further, I'll point out the differences between Java and Kotlin regarding statements and expressions. Some of these differences are as follows:

Assignments are **expressions in Java,** but they are **statements in Kotlin**. That means you cannot pass assignment operations as an argument to loop statements (like the *while* loop). Listing 2-2 shows an example of something you can do in Java but not in Kotlin.

Listing 2-2. Assignment operation as an argument to while

```
while ((rem = a % b) != 0) {
   a = b
   b = rem
}
println(b)
```

Kotlin won't let you compile the code sample above because the *while* statement expects an expression, and assignments are not expressions. Let's rewrite Listing 2-2 so it can work in Kotlin. (See Listing 2-3.)

Listing 2-3. Using the while loop in Kotlin

```
var foundGcf = false

while(!foundGcf) {
   rem = a % b
   if (rem != 0) {
      a = b
      b = rem
   }
   else {
      foundGcf = true
   }
}
println(b)
```

Another notable difference between Kotlin and Java regarding expressions and statements is that in Kotlin, most control structures (except *for, do, and do/while*) are expressions. At the same time, in Java, they are statements.

Keywords

Keywords are special or reserved words that have special meaning to the compiler, and as such, you cannot use them for identifiers (like class names, variable names, interface names, function names, etc.).

Kotlin has hard, soft, and modifier keywords. The hard keywords are always interpreted as keywords and cannot be used as identifiers. Some examples of these are *break, class, continue, do, else, false, while, this, throw, try, super,* and *when.*

Soft keywords act as reserved words in certain contexts where they are applicable; otherwise, they can be used as regular identifiers. Some examples of soft keywords are the following: *file, finally, get, import, receiver, set, constructor, delegate, get, by,* and *where.*

Lastly, there are modifier keywords. These things act as reserved words in a modifier list of declarations; otherwise, they can be used as identifiers. Some examples of these things are the following: *abstract, actual, annotation, companion, enum, final, infix, inline, lateinit, operator,* and *open.*

Tip   If you use IntelliJ, you don't have to memorize the list of keywords; the IDE will give you enough visual hints if you accidentally use a keyword as an identifier

---

Whitespace

Like Java, Kotlin is also a tokenized language. Whitespace is not significant and can be safely ignored. You can write your codes with extravagant use of whitespace, like this

```
fun                main(args: Array<String>) {
   println(       "Hello")
}
```

Or you can write it with very minimal whitespace, like the following example:

```
fun main(args: Array<String>) {println("Hello")}
```

Either way, the compiler doesn't care, so write your codes to benefit humans who may be unlucky enough to maintain our codes. Forget the compiler. It doesn't care about white space anyway. Use whitespaces to prettify the code and make it readable, probably something like this

```
fun main(args: Array<String>) {
   println("Hello")
}
```

Operators

Kotlin supports various operators and symbols we can use to formulate expressions and statements. Table 2-1 (below) shows some of them.

Table 2-1. *Kotlin operators and symbols*

Operators or symbols	What they mean
+, -, *, /, %	These are the usual Math operators; they do exactly what you expect them to do. No difference with Java at all. But we must note that in Kotlin, the asterisk or star symbol (*) is also used to pass an array to a vararg parameter.
=	The equal symbol is used for the assignment statement.
+=, -=, *=, /=, %=	These are augmented assignment operators. The += operator can be used like this a += 1 which is short for a = a + 1, the -= can be used like a -= 1, which is short for a = a -1, and so on.
&&, ||, ! logical "and", "or", "not" operators	You will use these operators when you need to construct complex or compound logical operations. The short-circuit *and* (&&) behaves similarly as in Java. When one of the operands evaluates to false, the other operand will no longer be evaluated, and the whole expression evaluates to false. While logical "and" does not perform short-circuit evaluation, think of it as the equivalent of the & operator in Java. The short-circuit or (||) acts the same as in Java. Kotlin doesn't have the single pipe operator; instead, it has the "or" operator—which performs a logical OR without short-circuiting.

(continued)

Table 2-1. (*continued*)

Operators or symbols	What they mean
==, !=	These are equality operators. Since Kotlin doesn't have primitive types (like in Java), you can use these operators to compare any type, basic or otherwise

```
fun main(args: Array<String>) {
    var a = "Hello"
    var b = "Hello"
```

```
if (a == b) { // this evaluates to true
    println("$a is equal to $b")
 }
}
```

In Java, we wouldn't be able to do object comparisons like this using the double equals operator. Objects (like *Strings*) should use the .equals() method if we want to test for equality. In Kotlin, however, we don't need to worry about such things. We use the double equals operator to compare *Strings*. Kotlin translates this internally to call to .equals() method

(*continued*)

Table 2-1. (*continued*)

Operators or symbols	What they mean
===, !===	The triple equals operation checks for referential equality (which is also true for its negated counterpart !==).
	The expression a===b evaluates to true if and only if variables *a* and *b* point to the same object. For example
	```\nvar p1 = Person("John")\nvar p2 = Person("John")\n\nif(p1 === p2) { // false\n println("p1 == p2")\n}\n```
	In the snippet above, *p1* and *p2* do not point to the same object; hence, the triple equals will not evaluate to true
<, >, <=, >=	Comparison operators. Kotlin translates these to calls to compareTo(). Kotlin doesn't have primitive types, remember?
[ ] [,]	You can use index access operators to get to the elements of a list or the values of a map, instead of using the Java-style get(index) or get(key).
	```\nfun main(args: Array<String>) {\n val fruits = listOf("Apple",\n "Banana", "Orange")\n println(fruits.get(2)) // Orange\n println(fruits[2]) // Orange\n}\n```

Blocks

Often, you'll need to write a bunch of statements and group them; you can do that by using blocks.

You can define a code block by using a pair of curly braces. You will find blocks in many Kotlin constructs like classes, functions, interfaces, loops, branches, etc. For example, to write a class, you may do it as follows:

```kotlin
class Person(val name: String) {

}
```

To define an interface, you can try something like this

```kotlin
interface Human {

  fun walk()
  fun talk()
}
```

To create a function, you may try something like this

```kotlin
fun main(args: Array<String>) {
  greet("John")
}

fun greet(name:String) {
  println("Hello $name")
}
```

To write a while loop, you might do it like this

```kotlin
var counter = 0
while (counter++ != 5) {
  println("counter $counter")
}
```

When using the *try-catch* construct

```
val num = "1"

val ans = try {
  Integer.parseInt(num)
}
catch(e:Exception) {
  e.printStackTrace()
}
```

And any other control structure that may need to group statements.

Comments

Comments are useless to the compiler. It ignores them. But comments are very helpful and useful to people. Comments excel at making our codes understandable. You can use comments to clarify and convey your intentions for the code.

There are three ways to write comments. You can use:

1. **Single-line comments**, also known as inline comments. These are written using two forward slashes. The compiler will ignore everything to the right of the slashes until the end of the line. See the example below:

   ```
   // This statement will be ignored
   var a = 0 // so will this line
   ```

2. **Multiline comments**, also known as C-style comments. They are called such because they came from the C language. This style is useful if your comments span multiple lines. See the example below:

```
/*
```

Everything inside the pair of these slashes
and asterisks will be ignored by the
compiler

```
*/
```

3. **KDoc** is like Javadoc, it starts with /**, and it ends
    with */. This form of comment is very similar
    to the multiline comment (above), but this is
    used to provide API documentation for Kotlin
    codes. Listing 2-4 (below) shows how to use the
    KDoc syntax.

Listing 2-4. KDoc syntax

```
/**
This is example documentation using KDoc syntax

@author Ted Hagos
@constructor
*/
class Person(val name: String) {
    /**
    This is another KDoc comment
    @return
    */
    fun foo(): Int{
      return 0
    }
}
```

Tip   You can comment multiple lines of code in IntelliJ by selecting the lines you want to comment on, then use the following keyboard shortcuts.

In Windows and Linux, these keys are

```
CTRL + / - comment using //
CTRL + Shift + / - comment using /* */
```

In macOS, the keys are

```
⌘ + / - comment using //
⌘ + ⌥ + / - comment using /* */
```

Basic Types

Kotlin has some basic types, but they are not the same as Java's primitive types because all types in Kotlin are objects. They're just called basic types because they are in very common usage. These types are *numbers, characters, booleans, arrays,* and *strings*—we'll look at them in this section.

Numbers and Literal Constants

There are built-in types to handle numbers (shown in Table 2-2). They appear as bona fide objects with member functions and properties. They may be represented as primitive values during runtime, but they don't appear to the programmer as primitives for all intents and purposes. Table 2-2 shows Kotlin's number built-in types.

Table 2-2. *Kotlin's number built-in types*

Type	Bit width
Double	64
Float	32
Long	64
Int	32
Short	16
Byte	8

Kotlin handles numbers very close to how Java handles them but with some notable differences. For example, widening conversions are not implicit anymore. You will need to perform the conversions deliberately:

```
var a = 10L // a is a Long literal, note the L postfix
var b = 20

var a = b // this won't work
var a = b.toLong() // this will work
```

When you use whole numbers as literal constants, they are automatically *Ints*. To declare a *Long* literal, use the L postfix, like so

```
var a = 100 // Int literal
var b = 10L // Long literal
```

You can use underscores in numeric literals to make them more readable. This feature is also available in Java (since Java 7 came out):

```
var oneMillion = 1_000_000
var creditCardNumber =  1234_5678_9012_3456
```

Literals with decimal positions are automatically *Doubles*. To declare a float literal, use the F postfix like in the following snippet:

```
var a = 3.1416 // Double literal
var b = 2.54F // Float literal
println(b::class.java.typeName) // prints float
println(a::class.java.typeName) //prints double
```

Every number type can be converted to any of the number types. All *Double, Float, Int, Long, Byte,* and *Short* types support the following member functions:

- toByte() : Byte
- toShort() : Short
- toInt() : Int
- toLong() : Long
- toFloat() : Float
- toDouble() : Double
- toChar() : Char

Characters

Characters in Kotlin cannot be treated directly as numbers. You can't do things like the following:

```
fun checkForKey(keyCode:Char) {
  if (keyCode == 97) { // won't work, keyCode is not a number
  }
}
```

Character literals are created by using single quotes, like so

```
var enterKey = 'a'
```

Like in Java, you can use escape sequences such as \t, \b, \n, \r, \', \", \\ and \$ and if you need to encode any other character, you can use the Unicode syntax, for example, \uFF00.

Let's not forget that *Characters* are objects in Kotlin, so you can call member functions on them. Listing 2-5 shows a snippet that demonstrates some usage scenarios.

Listing 2-5. Member functions of the Character type

```kotlin
val a = 'a'

println(a.isLowerCase()) // true
println(a.isDigit())     // false
println(a.toUpperCase()) // A

val b: String = a.toString() // converts it to a String
```

Booleans

Booleans are represented by the literals *true* and *false*. Kotlin doesn't have the notion of truthy and falsy values, like in other languages such as Python or JavaScript. It means that for constructs that expect a *Boolean* type, you have to supply either a *Boolean* literal, variable, or expression that will resolve to either true or false.

```kotlin
var count = 0

if (count) println("zero") // won't work
if ("") println("empty") // won't work either
var a = 1
var b = 1

if (a == b) println("a is equal to b") // this will print
if (a > b) println("a is greater than b") // this won't print
```

Arrays

Kotlin doesn't have an array object like the one created in Java using the square braces syntax. The Kotlin array is a generic class; it has a type parameter. We've been using Kotlin arrays for quite some time now because the small code snippets and the "Hello World" example in the previous chapter have featured the use of *Arrays*. The argument to the main function is actually an *Array* of *String*. Let's see that main function again, just as a refresher:

```
fun main(args:Array<String>) {


}
```

There are a couple of ways to create an array. They can be created using the arrayOf() and arrayOfNulls() built-in functions. You can also create arrays by using the *Array* constructor. Listing 2-6 provides some sample codes for working with them.

Listing 2-6. Working with the Array type

```
fun main(args: Array<String>) {
    var emptyArray = arrayOfNulls<String>(2)  ❶
    emptyArray[0] = "Hello"                    ❷
    emptyArray[1] = "World"

    for (i in emptyArray.indices) println(emptyArray[i])  ❸

    for (i in emptyArray) println(i)  ❹

    var arrayOfInts = arrayOf(1,2,3,4,5,6)  ❺
    arrayOfInts.forEach { e -> println(e) }  ❻
```

```
var arrayWords = "The quick brown fox".split(" ")
.toTypedArray() ❼
arrayWords.forEach { item -> println(item) }
}
```

❶ We used the arrayOfNulls function to create an array that has two elements.

❷ We can assign values to specific elements of the array. We just need to specify the element's position in the array using its index. This syntax of accessing the element of the array is the same as in Java.

❸ We can use the for loop to traverse the contents of the array. In this example, we used the indices to access the element of the array.

❹ This is a more direct way of accessing the element of the array. An Array object has an iterator, so we can use that iterator to get to the array element right away.

❺ This creates an array of Ints using the arrayOf() function.

❻ This example uses the forEach function to traverse the elements of the array. Using the forEach function is considered more idiomatic (and more efficient).

❼ This creates an array using an ArrayList(arrayWords). The List arrayWords was created by invoking the split() member function of the String.

Strings and String Templates

Much of what we've learned about Java Strings still applies in Kotlin.

The easiest way to create a String is to use the escaped string literal—escaped strings are actually the kind of strings we know from Java. These strings may contain escape characters like \n, \t, \b, etc. See the code snippet below:

```
var str: String = "Hello World\n"
```

Kotlin has another kind of string called a raw string; it's created using the triple quote delimiter. They may not contain escape sequences, but they can contain new lines, like this

```
var rawStr = """Amy Pond, there's something you'd
  better understand about me 'cause it's important,
  and one day your life may depend on it:
  I am definitely a mad man with a box!
  """
```

A couple more things we need to know about Kotlin strings are as follows:

1. They have iterators, so we can walk through the characters using a *for loop*

    ```
    val str = "The quick brown fox"
    for (i in str) println(i)
    ```

2. Its elements can be accessed by the indexing operator (str[elem]), pretty much like *Arrays*

    ```
    println(str[2]) // returns 'e'
    ```

3. We can no longer convert numbers (or anything else for that matter) to a String by simply adding an empty String literal to it

    ```
    var strNum =  10 + "" // this won't work anymore
    var strNum = 10.toString() // we have to explicitly
    convert now
    ```

We can still use String.format and System.out.printf in Kotlin; after all, we can use Java codes from within Kotlin. It's still possible to write programs like the code snippet shown in Listing 2-7.

Listing 2-7. Using String.format and printf

```
var name = "John Doe"
var email = "john.doe@gmail.com"
var phone = "(01)777-1234"

var concat = String.format("name: %s | email: %s | phone: %s",
name, email, phone)
println(concat)
// prints
// name: John Doe | email: john.doe@gmail.com | phone:
(01)777-1234
```

The preferred way to do string composition in Kotlin is by using string templates like this

```
var concat = "name: $name | email: $email | phone: $phone"
println(concat)
// prints
// name: John Doe | email: john.doe@gmail.com | phone:
(01)777-1234
```

Kotlin strings may contain template expressions; these are evaluated pieces of code. The result of the evaluation is inserted (concatenated) into the String. A template expression starts with a dollar sign ($) followed by an expression. See Listing 2-8 for examples.

Listing 2-8. Using template expressions

```
fun main(args:Array<String>) {
  var name = "John Doe"

  println("Hello $name") ❶
  println("The name '$name' is ${name.length} characters
  long") ❷
```

```
  println("Hello ${foo()}") ❸
}

fun foo(): String {
  return "Boo"
}
```

---

❶   Shows the basic use of a template string. The template expression is created
     using the $ symbol immediately followed by an identifier. The value of the
     identifier is evaluated, resolved, and finally inserted into the body of the String,
     where the template expression is declared.

❷   In this example, the name.length is enclosed in curly braces. This is
     because the $ symbol is right-associative. It will evaluate the expression that
     immediately follows it. That won't work in our situation because we don't
     want to evaluate the name variable. What we want to resolve instead is name.
     length. Hence, the need to enclose it in curly braces.

❸   We're not limited to simple variables; we can even write functions inside
     template expressions.

Controlling Program Flow

Program statements are executed sequentially by default, one after the
other, in a linear fashion. Some constructs can cause programs to deviate
from a linear flow. Some can cause the flow to fork or branch, and other
constructs can cause the program flow to go around in circles, like in a
loop. These constructs are the subject of this section.

Using ifs

The basic form of the *if* construct is as follows:

```
if (expression) statement
```

Where *expression* resolves to Boolean, the statement executes if the expression is true. Otherwise, the statement is ignored, and program control flows to the next executable statement. When you need to execute more than one statement, use a block with the *if* construct, like this

```
if (expression) {
    statements
}
```

Let's see how it looks in code

```
val theQuestion = "Doctor who"
val answer = "Theta Sigma"
val correctAnswer = ""

if (answer == correctAnswer) {
  println("You are correct")
}
```

So far, the *if* construct in Kotlin behaves exactly as it does in Java. It also supports the *else if* and the *else* clause, as shown in the following snippet:

```
val d = Date()
val c = Calendar.getInstance()
val day = c.get(Calendar.DAY_OF_WEEK)

if (day == 1) {
  println("Today is Sunday")
}
```

```
else if (day == 2) {
  println("Today is Monday")
}
else if ( day == 3) {
  println("Today is Tuesday")
}
```

The new thing about Kotlin's *if* is that it's an expression, which means we can do things like this

```
val theQuestion = "Doctor who"
val answer = "Theta Sigma"
val correctAnswer = ""

var message = if (answer == correctAnswer) {
  "You are correct"
}
else{
  "Try again"
}
```

The *String* on the first block of the *if* construct will be returned to the message variable if the condition is true. Otherwise, the *String* on the second block will be the returned value. We can even omit the curly braces on the blocks since the blocks contain only single statements:

```
var message = if (answer == correctAnswer) "You are correct"
else "Try again"
```

The preceding code example would probably remind you of the ternary operator in Java. By the way, Kotlin doesn't support the ternary operator but don't worry since you don't need it. The *if* construct is an expression. If you feel you need to write code that requires the ternary operator, just write something like the preceding code example.

The when Statement

Kotlin doesn't have a *switch* statement, but it has the *when* construct. Its form and structure are strikingly similar to the *switch* statement. In its simplest form, it can be implemented like this

```
val d = Date()
val c = Calendar.getInstance()
val day = c.get(Calendar.DAY_OF_WEEK)

when (day) {
  1 -> println("Sunday")
  2 -> println("Monday")
  3 -> println("Tuesday")
  4 -> println("Wednesday")
}
```

When will try to match the argument (the variable *day*) against all branches sequentially until it hits a match; note that unlike in *switch* statements, when a match is found, it doesn't flow through or cascade to the next branch; hence we don't need to put a *break* statement.

The *when* construct can also be used as an expression, and when it's used as such, each branch becomes the returned value of the expression. See the code example below:

```
val d = Date()
val c = Calendar.getInstance()
val day = c.get(Calendar.DAY_OF_WEEK)

var dayOfweek = when (day) {
  1 -> "Sunday"
  2 -> "Monday"
  3 -> "Tuesday"
```

```
    4 -> "Wednesday"
    else -> "Unknown"
}
```

Just remember to include the *else* clause if you use *when* as an expression. The compiler thoroughly checks all possible pathways and needs to be exhaustive, which is why the *else* clause becomes a requirement.

You're not limited to numeric literals. You can use various data types for the branches, as shown in Listing 2-9.

Listing 2-9. How to write branches inside the when construct

```
fun main(args: Array<String>) {

  print("What is the answer to life? ")
  var response:Int? = readLine()?.toInt() ❶

  val message = when(response){
    42 -> "So long, and thanks for the all fish"
    43, 44, 45 -> "either 43,44 or 45" ❷
    in 46 .. 100 ->  "forty six to one hundred" ❸
    else -> "Not what I'm looking for" ❹
  }

  println(message)
}
```

---

❶ readLine() reads input from the console. Don't worry about the questions marks; for now, we'll get to that in the coming sections.

❷ The branch conditions may be combined with a comma.

❸ We can check if it's a member of a range or a collection.

❹ The *else* clause is required if you use *when* as an expression.

The while Statement

The *while* and *do . . while* statements work exactly as they do in Java—and like in Java, these are also statements and not expressions. We won't spend too much time on *while* and *do . . while* loops here.

Basic usage of the while loop is shown below, just as a refresher:

```
fun main(args: Array<String>) {
  var count = 0
  val finish = 5

  while (count++ < finish) {
    println("counter = $count")
  }
}
```

for Loops

Kotlin doesn't have the older style *for loop* of Java 7 (and below)—the one that looks like the following:

```
for (int i = 0; i < 10; i++) {
  statements
}
```

Kotlin's *for loop* works on things that have an iterator. If you've seen the *for each* loop in JavaScript, C#, or Java 8 (and higher), Kotlin's for loop is closer to that. A basic example is shown in Listing 2-10.

Listing 2-10. Basic for loop

```
fun main(args: Array<String>) {
  val words:List = "The quick brown fox".split(" ") ❶

  for(word in words) { ❷
    println(word) ❸
  }
}
```

---

❶   The split() method of the String class returns a *List* type. We can iterate over that

❷   For each item (word) in the collection (words), we

❸   Print the item

If you need to work with numbers on the *for loop*, you can use *Ranges*. A range is a type that represents an arithmetic progression of integers. Ranges are created with the rangeTo() function, but we usually use it in its operator form (. .). To create a range of integers from 0 to 10, we write it like this

```
var zeroToTen = 0..10
```

We can use the *in* keyword to perform a test of membership

```
if (9 in zeroToTen) println("9 is in zeroToTen")
```

To use *ranges* in for loops, we can start with something that looks like the code shown in Listing 2-11.

Listing 2-11. Using ranges in for loop

```
fun main(args: Array<String>) {
  for (i in 1..10) {
    println(i)
  }
}
```

Exception Handling

Kotlin's exception handling is very similar to Java. It also uses the *try-catch-finally* construct. Whatever we've learned about Java's exception handling commutes nicely to Kotlin. However, Kotlin simplifies exception handling by simply using unchecked exceptions. What that means is, writing *try-catch* blocks is now optional. You may or may not do it. Consider the code shown in Listing 2-12.

Listing 2-12. I/O operations without try-catch blocks

```
import java.io.FileReader ❶

fun main(args: Array<String>) {

  var fileReader = FileReader("README.txt") ❷

  var content = fileReader.read() ❸
  println(content)

}
```

---

❶   We can use Java's standard library in Kotlin.

❷   This one may throw the *"FileNotFoundException"*.

❸   And this could throw the *"IOException"*, but Kotlin happily lets us code without handling the possible *Exceptions* that may be thrown.

Although Kotlin lets us avoid handling exceptions, we can still do that (and we may have to in some situations). When that happens, just write the exception handling code the way you did in Java. See Listing 2-13 for an example.

Listing 2-13. Kotlin's try-catch block

```kotlin
import java.io.FileNotFoundException
import java.io.FileReader
import java.io.IOException

fun main(args: Array<String>) {

  var fileReader: FileReader

  try {
    fileReader = FileReader("README.txt")
    var content = fileReader.read()
    println(content)
  }
  catch (ffe: FileNotFoundException) {
    println(ffe.message)
  }
  catch(ioe: IOException) {
    println(ioe.message)
  }
}
```

Handling Nulls

A common source of bugs and expensive rework activities in Java may be attributed to how programmers handle null values. Some of us are diligent and such defensive programmers that this discussion may not be necessary anymore. Most of the time, we need to be reminded of the possibility of *NullPointerExceptions*. Handling null values is such a big concern in Java that Kotlin made a deliberate decision to introduce the concept of a *Nullable* type. In Kotlin, when we declare a variable like so

```
var str: String = "Hello"
str = null // won't work
```

We will never be able to set the value of this variable to null. We may assign it a different *String* value, but Kotlin guarantees that str will never be null. If for some reason, you really need this variable to be null, you have to explicitly tell Kotlin that str is a *Nullable* type. To make a *String* (or any type) Nullable, we use the question mark symbol as a postfix to the type, like this

```
var str: String? = "Hello"
```

After declaring a type as *Nullable*, we now have to do some things that Kotlin used to do for us. For non-*Nullable* types, Kotlin ensures that it's pretty safe to use them in operations such as assignment, printing, inclusion in expressions, etc. When we make types *Nullable*, Kotlin assumes that we know what we're doing and that we're responsible enough to write the necessary guard conditions to prevent *NullPointerExceptions*. Kotlin assumes we'd do something like the code shown in Listing 2-14.

Listing 2-14. Demonstration of Nullable types

```
fun main(args: Array<String>) {
  var a = arrayOf(1,2,3)
  printArr(null)
}
```

```
fun printArr(arr: Array<Int>?) {  ❶
  if(arr != null) {  ❷
    arr.forEach { i -> println(i) }  ❸
  }
}
```

---

❶   We're declaring Array<Int> to be Nullable. This means we can pass null to printArr().

❷   Because arr is no longer guaranteed to be non-null, we have to manually check for null values before we do some operations which involve the arr local variable.

❸   If arr is not null, we can safely perform this operation.

Kotlin introduced an operator that we can use to handle *Nullable* types. It's called the safe-call operator, which is written as the question mark symbol followed by a dot "?."

We can replace the entire if block that performs the null checking with just one statement:

```
arr?.forEach { i -> println(i) }
```

The safe call first checks if *arr* is null. If it is, it won't go through the *forEach* operation. The array is traversed only when *arr* is not null.

Listing 2-15 shows the refactored code for Listing 2-14.

Listing 2-15. Safe call operator

```
fun main(args: Array<String>) {
  var a = arrayOf(1,2,3)
  printArr(null)
}
```

```
fun printArr(arr: Array<Int>?) {
   arr?.forEach { i -> println(i) }
}
```

Kotlin's default behavior regarding the nullability of objects should prevent many of us from doing things that will disgrace us because it doesn't allow variables to be null by default. However, if we think we know what we're doing and certain situations would force us to use *Nullable* types, we can still do that. Just remember to use the safe call operator; it's idiomatic compared to performing null checks using *ifs*.

Key Takeaways

- Kotlin's program elements are not very different from Java. It also has operators, blocks, statements, expressions, etc. However, some constructs that are considered statements in Java are expressions in Kotlin, and some that were considered expressions in Java are statements in Kotlin, for example, the assignment operation.

- Kotlin's basic types are not the same as primitive types of Java. Everything in Kotlin is an object.

- There are two ways to declare a variable in Kotlin. When the var keyword is used, the variable is mutable. When the val keyword is used, the variable is immutable.

- Strings in Kotlin have iterators. Also, they're easier to compose and combine with the help of template expressions.

- When variables are declared in Kotlin, they are, by default, non-Nullable, unless we declare them otherwise.

- Kotlin doesn't have a *switch* statement, but it's got the *when* construct.

- Kotlin uses unchecked Exceptions by default. That's why exception handling is optional.

CHAPTER 3

Functions

If you're coming from Java programming, a named collection of statements is called a method. In Kotlin, we call them functions. But Kotlin functions are more than just a named collection of statements. Kotlin functions are first-class citizens. You can use a function wherever you can use a variable. You can pass them as parameters to other functions and return functions from other functions as well; this is what makes functional programming possible in Kotlin; it supports higher order functions. But before we can dive into that topic, we need to start with the basics of Kotlin functions, for example, how they are declared, how they treat parameters, how different (or similar) they are from Java methods, plus a couple of other details.

What we'll cover:

- Declaring functions

- Default parameters

- Named parameters

- Extension functions

- Infix functions

- Infix operators

© Ted Hagos 2023
T. Hagos, *Beginning Kotlin*, https://doi.org/10.1007/978-1-4842-8698-2_3

Declaring Functions

You can write functions in three places. You can place them

1. Inside a class. These are called member functions

2. Outside a class. These are called top-level functions

3. Inside other functions. These are called local functions

Regardless of where you place your functions, the mechanics of declaring them doesn't change much. The basic form of a function is as follows:

```
fun functionName([parameters]) [:type] {
  statements
}
```

You declare the function using the reserved word *fun* followed by an identifier (the function's name).

The function name includes the parenthesis, where you can define optional parameters. You may also define the type of data the function will return (if it returns any), but this is optional since Kotlin can infer the function's return type by simply looking at its body declaration. After writing the function's name, you will write a pair of curly braces to enclose the function's body.

It's a good idea to follow Java's guidelines for naming identifiers when naming your Kotlin functions. Function names

1. Should not be a reserved word

2. Must not start with a number

3. Should not have special characters in them

4. As much as possible, should contain a verb or something signifying an action—as opposed to when naming a variable where the variable **name** contains a noun

Listing 3-1 shows a basic declaration of functions that takes a String and Int parameters. For comparison purposes, Listing 3-3 shows the equivalent Java code for Listing 3-1.

You should name your functions following the same guidelines as if you are writing Java methods; namely, the function name (1) shouldn't be a reserved word, (2) must not start with a number, and (3) shouldn't have special characters in them. And lastly, from a stylistic perspective, its name should contain a verb or something signifying an action—as opposed to when you are naming a variable where the name contains a noun. Listing 3-1 shows a basic declaration of a Kotlin function that takes a *String* and *Int* parameters. If you want to look at the Java equivalent, I wrote an example in Listing 3-3.

Listing 3-1. displayMessage function

```
fun displayMessage(msg: String, count: Int) {
  var counter = 1
  while(counter++ <= count ) {
    println(msg)
  }
}
```

The displayMessage() in Listing 3-1 is a non-productive function. It doesn't return anything.

In Java, when a function doesn't return anything, we still indicate that the return type is void (see Listing 3-3). In Kotlin, however, we don't have to do that since it is capable of type inference; it can figure out the return type for itself. But let's rewrite Listing 3-1 verbosely to ultimately tell the compiler what kind of return type displayMessage() has. See Listing 3-2.

Listing 3-2. displayMessage with an explicit return type

```
fun displayMessage(msg: String, count: Int) : Unit {
  var counter = 1
  while(counter++ <= count ) {
    println(msg)
  }
}
```

The only difference between Listings 3-1 and 3-2 is the *Unit* return type of the displayMessage() function. *Unit* corresponds to Java's *void*.

Listing 3-3. DisplayMessage in Java

```
public class DisplayMessage {

  public static void main(String []args) {
    displayMessage("Hello", 3);
  }

  static void displayMessage(String msg, int count) {
    int counter = 1;
    while(counter++ <= count) {
      System.out.println(msg);
    }
  }
}
```

If you want to run the displayMessage() function, you can call it by its name and pass the proper parameters, as shown in Listing 3-4.

Listing 3-4. Calling the displayMessage function

```
fun main(args: Array<String>) {
  displayMessage("Hello", 3) ❶ ❷
}

fun displayMessage(msg: String, count: Int) {
  var counter = 1
  while(counter++ <= count ) {
    println(msg)
  }
}
```

❶ "Hello" is passed to the *msg* argument of displayMessage().

❷ 3 is passed to the *count* argument of displayMessage(); like in Java, arguments passed to a function are matched to its parameters in the order they were defined, starting from left going to the right.

To make functions productive (returns something), just put a *return* statement somewhere in the function's body and declare the function's return type. See Listing 3-5 for an example.

Listing 3-5. getSum, a productive function

```
fun main(args: Array<String>) {
  println(getSum(listOf(1,2,3,4,5,6)))
}

fun getSum(values: List<Int>) : Int { // return type is Int
  var total = 0;
```

```
  for (i in values)  total += i
  return total                                    // return value
}
```

You can return anything from functions; we're not limited to the basic types. See Listing 3-6 for a code example.

Listing 3-6. Using Pairs as a return type

```
fun bigSmall(a: Int, b:Int) : Pair<Int, Int> { ❶

  if(a > b) return Pair(a,b) ❷
  else {
    return Pair(b,a) ❸
  }
}

fun main(args: Array<String>) {
  var (x,y) = bigSmall(5,3) ❹

  println(x)
  println(y)
}
```

---

❶   The bigSmall() function tells the compiler that it returns a *Pair*. A *Pair* is a data class that represents, well, a generic pair. If you've used Python before, this might remind you of tuples. In Java, you the closest data structure is the Pair (found in javafx.util package).

❷   If parameter *a* is greater than *b*, then we create the *Pair* using parameter *a* as the first component and *b* as the second component, then we return it to the caller.

❸   If parameter *a* is less than *b*, then we create the *Pair* using parameter *b* as the first component and *a* as the second component, and then we return it to the caller.

❹   A Pair can be returned to two named variables on the left-hand side of the assignment statement. This destructuring declaration allows us to save multiple values to multiple variables simultaneously. In this case, variable *x* will receive the first component of the returned Pair, and variable *y* will receive the second component of the *Pair*

Single Expression Functions

Earlier in the chapter, we did say that functions follow the basic form

```
fun functionName([parameters]) [:type] {
    statements
}
```

There is another way to write Kotlin functions that lets us get away with fewer codes.

There are times when you can omit (1) the *return* statement, (2) curly braces, and (3) the *return type* altogether. This second form of writing a function is called *single expression* function. You can probably guess from its name that the function only contains a single expression, as shown in the code snippet below:

```
fun sumInt(a: Int, b: Int) = a + b
```

A single expression function omits the pair of curly braces. Instead of the braces, the function uses an assignment operator. It also doesn't need the return statement anymore because the expression on the right-hand side of the assignment automatically becomes the returned value. Finally, a function like this doesn't need an explicit return type because the compiler can infer the type returned from the value of the expression. The omission of the explicit return type is not, in any way, a hard rule. You may still write an explicit return if that's what you prefer, like in the following:

```kotlin
fun sumInt(a: Int, b: Int): Int = a + b
```

Default Arguments

Function parameters can have default values in Kotlin, which lets the caller (of the function) skip some arguments on the call site. You can add a default to a function's signature by assigning a value to its parameter. See Listing 3-7 for an example.

Listing 3-7. connectToDb

```kotlin
fun connectToDb(hostname: String = "localhost",
                username: String = "mysql",
                password:String = "secret") {
}
```

Notice that "localhost", "mysql", and "secret" were assigned to hostname, username, and password, respectively. You can call the function like this

```kotlin
connectToDb("mycomputer","root")
```

I didn't pass the third argument in the code snippet above, but that is still a valid call because all of the function's parameters have default values. I can even call the function without passing any argument at all like this

```kotlin
connectToDb()
```

With default arguments, you won't need to use method overloads anymore—although you can still do function overloading in Kotlin, you probably have less reason to do it because of default parameters.

Named Parameters

Let's go back to Listing 3-7 (previous section). If we call the `connectToDb()` function and pass all the arguments, the call looks like the following:

```
connectToDb("neptune", jupiter", "saturn")
```

Can you spot the problem? That is a valid call because all parameters of `connectToDb()` are *Strings*, and we passed three *String* arguments. It isn't clear from the call site which one is the username, the hostname, or the password. In Java, this ambiguity problem is solved by various workarounds, including commenting on the call site like this

```
connectoToDb(/* hostname*/, "neptune,
             /* username*/ "jupiter",
             /*password*/ "saturn")
```

We don't have to do this in Kotlin because we can name the argument at the call site like this

```
connecToDb(hostname = "neptune",
           username = "jupiter",
           password = "saturn")
```

You must remember that when you start to specify the argument name, you need to specify the names of all the following arguments to avoid confusion; besides, Kotlin won't let you compile such codes. For example, if we did something like the following:

```
connectToDb(hostname = "neptune",
            username = "jupiter",
            "saturn")
```

63

That isn't allowed because once we name the second argument (*username*), we need to provide the name of all the arguments that come after it. And in the example above, the second argument is named but not the third one. On the other hand, a call like the following:

```
connectToDb("neptune",
            username = "jupiter",
            password = "saturn")
```

Is allowed. It's okay that we didn't name the first argument because Kotlin treats it as a regular call and uses the positional value of the argument to resolve the parameter. Then we named all the remaining arguments.

Variable Number of Arguments

Functions in Kotlin, like in Java, can also accept an arbitrary number of arguments (varargs). The syntax is slightly different from Java; instead of using three dots after the type ..., we use the *vararg* keyword. Listing 3-8 shows examples of how to declare (and call) a *vararg* function.

Listing 3-8. Demonstration of a variable argument function

```
fun<T> manyParams(vararg va : T) { ❶
  for (i in va) { ❷
    println(i)
  }
}

fun main(args: Array<String>) {
  manyParams(1,2,3,4,5) ❸
  manyParams("From", "Gallifrey", "to", "Trenzalore") ❹
  manyParams(*args) ❺
  manyParams(*"Hello there".split(" ").toTypedArray())❻
}
```

❶ You can use the *vararg* keyword to accept multiple parameters for the manyParams() function. In the example, the function has a typed parameter. It's generic. We didn't have to use generics to work with variable arguments, but we chose to so the function can work with a variety of types.

❷ This is a simple looping mechanism so we can print each item in the argument.

❸ We can pass *Ints*, and we can pass as many as we want because the manyParams() function accepts a variable number of arguments.

❹ The function works with Strings as well.

❺ Like in Java, we can pass an array to a function that accepts variable arguments. We need to use the spread operator (*) to unpack the array. It's like passing the individual elements of the array one by one, manually.

❻ The split() member function will return an *ArrayList*. You can convert it to an *Array*, then use the spread operator so you can pass it to a *vararg* function.

Extension Functions

In Java, if we needed to add functionality to a class, we could either add methods to the class itself or extend it by inheritance, then add the new method to the child class. An *extension function* in Kotlin lets us add behavior to an existing class (including ones written in Java) without using inheritance. It lets us define a function that can be invoked as a class member, but the function is implemented outside the class.

To demonstrate this, let's start with a simple code (shown in Listing 3-9). It's a contrived application, but it should set the grounds for us to explore extension functions.

Listing 3-9. homerify, chanthofy, terminatorify

```
fun main(args: Array<String>) {
  val msg = "My name is Maximus Decimus Meridius"
  println(homerify(msg))
  println(chanthofy(msg))
  println(terminatorify(msg))

}

fun homerify(msg: String) = "$msg -- woohoo!"
fun chanthofy(msg: String) = "Chan, $msg , tho"
fun terminatorify(msg: String) = "$msg -- I'll be back"
```

The code in Listing 3-9 has three functions that take a String argument, add some Strings to it, and then return them to the caller; it's simple. The functions are usable as they stand, but we can consolidate a bit more by putting all three functions (homerify, chantofy, and terminatorify) in a single class (which becomes our utility class). Listing 3-10 shows the reworked utility class.

Listing 3-10. Our very own StringUtil class

```
fun main(args: Array<String>) {
  val msg = "My name is Maximus Decimus Meridius"

  val util = StringUtil()
  println(util.homerify(msg))
  println(util.chanthofy(msg))
  println(util.terminatorify(msg))
}

/*
  The StringUtil class consolidates our 3 methods as member
  functions.
```

```
  This is a very common Java practice
*/
class StringUtil {
    fun homerify(msg: String) = "$msg -- woohoo!"
    fun chanthofy(msg:String) = "Chan, $msg , tho"
    fun terminatorify(msg: String) = "$msg -- I'll be back"
}
```

Listing 3-10 looks familiar now; this is a very common practice in Java. It's considered a good idea to consolidate related methods into a utility class. Although Java programmers might have implemented homerify(), chanthofy(), and terminatorify() as static methods and not instance methods, as we did here, that's a small matter, and we can safely ignore it. The point is, in Kotlin, instead of writing a utility class for our three methods, we can rewrite our methods in a much simpler way. Listing 3-11 shows us how.

Listing 3-11. homerify as an extension function

```
fun String.homerify() = "$this -- woohoo!"
```

The code snippet above looks deceptively simple, but this is really all it takes to write an extension function.

Extension functions introduce the concept of a *receiver* type and a *receiver* object. In Listing 3-11, the *receiver* type is *String*—it's the class to which we'd like to add our extension function. The *receiver* object is the instance of that type, which in our example is "*My name is Maximus Decimus Meridius*". When you attach an extension function to a type, such as a *String* in our case, the extension function can reference the receiver object using the keyword *this*.

An extension function appears just like any member function defined on the *receiver* type. So, it makes sense for the extension function to be able to reference *this*. Listing 3-12 shows the full code for our extended String class.

Listing 3-12. Extended String class

```
fun main(args: Array<String>) {
  val msg = "My name is Maximus Decimus Meridius"

  println(msg.homerify())
  println(msg.chanthofy())
  println(msg.terminatorify())

}

fun String.homerify() = "$this -- woohoo!"
fun String.chanthofy() = "Chan, $this , tho"
fun String.terminatorify() = "$this -- I'll be back"
```

It's perfectly fine to still write utility functions in Kotlin. Still, with extension functions at our disposal, it seems more natural to use them because it increases the semantic value of the code. It feels more natural to use extension function syntax.

Infix Functions

Infix notation is one of the notations used in math and logical expressions. It's the placement of the operator between operands, for example, *a* + *b*. The plus symbol is infixed because it's between the operands *a* and *b*. In contrast, operations can follow postfixed notation where the expression is written like so *(+ a b)*, or they can be postfixed in which our expression is written like this *(a b +)*.

In Kotlin, member functions can be infixed, which lets us write codes like the following:

```
john say "Hello World"
```

If *john* is a variable that points to an object of type *Person* (we'll see the definition in a little while) and *say* is a method that takes a *String* argument like "Hello World", then the statement above is a more natural way of writing something like this

```
john.say("Hello World")
```

To begin our exploration of infix functions, let's implement the codes that will let us call the say() member function using the traditional dot notation; then, let's write the code that will use the infixed version. Listing 3-13 shows the classic implementation of the *Person* class, which uses dot notation.

Listing 3-13. Person class without infix function

```
fun main(args: Array<String>) {
  val john = Person("John Doe")
  john.say("Hello World")
}

class Person(val name : String) {
  fun say(message: String) = println("$name is saying
  $message")
}
```

No surprises there. This is OOP 101 programming. The example above does not need any further explanation. It is plain. It is obvious. Now, let's see the implementation that lets us call the *say* method in an "infixed" way.

Listing 3-14. Person class with an infix function

```
fun main(args: Array<String>) {
  val john = Person("John Doe")
  john say "Hello World"
}
```

```
class Person(val name : String) {
  infix fun say(message: String) = println("$name is saying
  $message")
}
```

The only thing you need to call the say() function in an infixed way is to add the *infix* keyword at the beginning of the function, as shown in Listing 3-14. Having said that, you cannot convert every function to become infix. A function can be converted to infix only if

- It is a member function (part of a class) or an extension function.

- It accepts no more than one parameter. If you're thinking of a loophole like, "I could probably define a single parameter in my function and use vararg"—that won't work. Variable arguments are not allowed on infix functions.

By the way, you cannot call an infix function using named parameters, like in the following:

```
john say msg = "Hello World" // won't work
```

Remember that infix functions take only a single argument; it doesn't make much sense to name the argument at the call site.

Infix functions, when used judiciously, allow for more intuitive coding because they can hide program logic behind a keyword-like syntax. You can create some sort of a meta-language with infix notation; just be careful not to overdo it.

Operator Overloading

Operator overloading might seem out of place in a chapter about functions, but in Kotlin, operator overloading is related to the discussion of functions. A discussion of operator overloading makes sense after a discussion of infix functions because the two have shared mechanics in implementation.

Operator overloading lets us appropriate the use of some standard operators, like math's *addition, subtraction, division, multiplication,* and *modulo.* For example, we can write a code that lets us use the plus sign to add two *Employee* objects or any other custom type. Consider the code in Listing 3-15.

Listing 3-15. Adding two Employee objects

```
fun main(args: Array<String>) {

  var e1 = Employee("John Doe")
  var e2 = Employee("Jane Doe")
  var e3 = e1 + e2
  println(e3.name)
}
```

Somehow, we intuitively know what the statement e3 = e1 + e2 means. If we add one employee object to another, then we should get the combined information or state of employees *e1* and *e2*—if that is the kind of thing you want to be able to do in code. Programmatically, we know this statement should not work because the addition operator doesn't know anything about Employee objects, much less how to perform the addition operation on them. However, in Kotlin, we can teach the addition operator how to add two Employee objects; this is shown in Listing 3-16.

Listing 3-16. class Employee

```
class Employee(var name: String) {

    infix operator  fun plus(emp: Employee) : Employee { ❶
      this.name += "\n${emp.name}"
      return this
  }
}
```

---

❶   This syntax is very similar to an infix function, as seen in the previous section. The only thing new here is the operator keyword.

We already know what the infix keyword will do to the function. The fact that *plus* is an *infixed* function allows us to write code like this (see Listing 3-16)

```
var e1 = Employee("John Doe")
var e2 = Employee("Jane Doe")

var e3 = e1 plus e2
```

However, the function name *plus* isn't an ordinary function name. It isn't just another name that we thought about and made up. It has a special meaning to Kotlin. The *plus* function name is a *fixed identifier* corresponding to the math operator +. When this special function name is combined with the keywords *infix* and *operator*, it lets us write codes like this

```
var e3 = e1 + e2
```

In Kotlin, we can override many operators, and we're not limited to just math operators. Table 3-1 shows some of them. It's not a complete list, but it should give you an idea of how much you can overload. For more information, you can visit https://kotlinlang.org/docs/operator-overloading.html.

Table 3-1. *Operators that can be overloaded and their corresponding function names*

Operator	Function name	Expression	Translated to
+	Plus	a + b	a.plus(b)
-	minus	a - b	a.minus(b)
/	div	a / b	a.div(b)
*	times	a * b	a.times(b)
%	rem	a % b	a.rem(b)
..	rangeTo	a .. b	a.rangeTo(b)
++	inc	a++	a.inc()
--	dec	a--	a.dec()
+=	plusAssign	a += b	a.plusAssign(b)
-+	minusAssign	a -= b	a.minusAssign(b)
/=	divAssign	a /= b	a.divAssign(b)
*=	timesAssign	a *= b	a.timesAssign(b)
%=	remAssign	a %= b	a.remAssign(b)
>	compareTo	a > b	a.compareTo(b) > 0
<	compareTo	a < b	a.conpareTo(b) < 0
>=	compareTo	a >=	a.conpareTo(b) >= 0
<=	compareTo	a<= b	a.conpareTo(b) <= 0

Operator overloading is a specific case of polymorphism where different operators, like math operators, can have different implementations depending on the arguments (or type of operands). When done correctly, the use of operator overloading lets us write codes that are easier to understand because they are written in the *business* or *object domain language*. They have higher semantic values.

Kotlin isn't the first language to implement operator overloading. It's been done by languages like C++ before. It should be noted that the use, or more aptly, the overuse and abuse of operator overloading, has led to much criticism. Precisely because if you can redefine the actions and behavior or well-known operators like plus, minus, etc. It can lead to unwieldy code. So, exercise good judgment when you use *operator overloading*.

Key Takeaways

- You can write functions in three places. Like in Java, they can be a member of the class, but you can also write them as a top-level construct. Thirdly, they can be written and embedded in other functions—we did not deal with local functions in this chapter, but we will consider this topic with some length in later chapters.

- Kotlin makes it easier to declare and call functions by adding support for default parameters, named parameters, and even variable number of arguments. The combination of positional, named, and default parameters allows us to move away from excessive use of parametric overloading, like what we did in Java.

- Extension functions offer a new way to extend behaviors of existing types. We can add the extra behavior outside the class, but we can call the extension function as if it was baked right into the class definition.

- Infix functions and operators let us increase the semantic values of our codes by allowing us to write function invocations without using dot notation. By allowing function calls to be *infix*-ed, the resulting code becomes more expressive and closer to the language of the domain.

CHAPTER 4

Types

Kotlin is a class-based, object-oriented language. It uses interfaces and classes to define custom types. If you're coming from Java (or any other similar language), you'll be at home with how Kotlin deals with data types because they are very similar.

What we'll cover:

- Interfaces
- Classes
- Data classes
- Inheritance modifiers
- Object declarations

Interfaces

Kotlin lets you define a type via interfaces. Its basic form looks like the following (Listing 4-1).

Listing 4-1. interface Fax

```
interface Fax {
  fun call(number: String) = println("Calling $number")
  fun print(doc: String) = println("Fax:Printing $doc")
  fun answer()
}
```

© Ted Hagos 2023
T. Hagos, *Beginning Kotlin*, https://doi.org/10.1007/978-1-4842-8698-2_4

Kotlin (like Java) uses the *interface* keyword and may contain *abstract* function(s). What's remarkable about Kotlin interfaces is that they can (1) contain properties and (2) have functions with implementations—concrete functions, in other words.

Kotlin uses the colon operator to implement an interface, as shown in the code Listing below. Listing 4-2 shows the MultiFunction class, which implements the Fax interface we defined in Listing 4-1.

Listing 4-2. class MultiFunction implementing Fax

```
class MultiFunction : Fax { ❶
  override fun answer() { ❷

  }
}
```

---

❶   We use the colon operator instead of Java's *implements* keyword. We use the colon for class inheritance as well.

❷   We have to provide an implementation for the answer() function because it didn't have an implementation in the Fax interface definition. On the other hand, we don't have to provide an implementation for call() and print() because these functions have implementations in the interface definition. You may also note that we are using the *override* keyword in this function because we need to tell the compiler that we don't intend to hide or overshadow the answer() function in the interface definition. Rather, we want to replace it, so it can be polymorphic. We want to provide our behavior for the answer() function in the MultiFunction class.

Why would Kotlin let us write concrete implementations within interfaces? Aren't *interfaces* supposed to contain only *abstract functions* and leave the implementations to the classes that will implement the *interface*? That way, you can enforce contracts between types. In the early days of Java, that was precisely the way interfaces behaved; they were purely an *abstract construction*. However, as of Java 8, you can already provide *default implementations* on *interfaces*.

There are some practical reasons for allowing implementations in interfaces; this lets us evolve interfaces over time. Imagine if we wrote *interface Foo* today with member functions a(), b(), and c(), and then we released it to other developers. In the future, if we add function *d()* to *interface Foo*, all codes that use *Foo* will now break. However, if we provide a *default implementation* for *d()*, the existing codes don't have to break. This is one of the use cases where a function implementation on an interface could be useful.

Diamond Problem

A *"diamond problem"* happens when a class inherits from two (or more) super types, and both super types implement the same function or method. Listing 4-3 shows an example of this.

Listing 4-3. Diamond problem

```
interface A {
  fun foo() {
    println("A:foo")
  }
}

interface B {
  fun foo() {
    println("B:foo")
  }
}

class Child : A, B {

}
```

The previous code sample will not compile because it is unclear what the result will be if we invoke function foo() against an instance of Child class. We declared function foo() in both interfaces A and B, which both have default implementation for the function—this is known as the "diamond problem". It happens When you have a class inheriting from at least two supertypes, and both supertypes have implementation for the duplicated function. To resolve the problem, we need to override the inherited function (the one that's duplicated in the supertypes) within the Child class. Listing 4-4 shows the solution.

Listing 4-4. How to solve the diamond problem

```kotlin
interface A {
  fun foo() {
    println("A:foo")
  }
}

interface B {
  fun foo() {
    println("B:foo")
  }
}

class Child : A, B {
  override fun foo () {
    println("Child:foo")
  }
}

fun main(args: Array<String>) {
  var child: Child = Child()
  child.foo()
}
```

Invoking Super Behavior

Kotlin's functions can call the functions defined on its supertype if it has an implementation; similar to Java, Kotlin uses the *super* keyword to do this. The *super* keyword is a reference to the instance of the *supertype*.

To invoke a function on a supertype, you'll need three things: (1) the *super* keyword, (2) the name of the supertype enclosed in a pair of angle brackets, and (3) the name of the function you want to call on the supertype. It looks something like the code snippet as follows:

```
super<NameOfSuperType>.functionName()
```

Let's expand our Fax and Multifunction example from earlier in the chapter. Listing 4-5 shows the revised code.

Listing 4-5. Printable, Fax, and MultiFunction

```
interface Printable {
  fun print(doc:String) = println("Printer:Printing $doc")
}

interface Fax {
  fun call(number: String) = println("Calling $number")
  fun print(doc: String) = println("Fax:Printing $doc")
  fun answer() = println("answering")
}

class MultiFunction : Printable, Fax {

  override fun print(doc:String)  {
    println("Multifunction: printing")
  }
}
```

Listing 4-5 shows the Fax and MultiFunction example from earlier. We've added a new interface called *Printable,* which also defines a print() function. The *MultiFunction* class inherits from both *Fax* and the new *Printable* interface, and it also overrides the print() function—it has to because the print() function is inherited from both *Printable* and *Fax* interfaces and default implementations exist on both supertypes.

The overridden print() function in *MultiFunction* has a simple *println* statement. To demonstrate how to call a function on the supertype, we will invoke the print() function on both supertypes from within the overridden print() in the *MultiFunction* class. Listing 4-6 shows us how to do this.

Listing 4-6. MultiFunction, calling functions on supertype

```
class MultiFunction : Printable, Fax {

  override fun print(doc:String)  {
    super<Fax>.print(doc)
    super<Printable>.print(doc)
    println("Multifunction: printing")
  }
}
```

When we call print(), it will run the print() function in *Fax,* then in *Printable,* and finally, whatever statements are left in the overridden print() of the *MultiFunction* class. Listing 4-7 shows the fully reworked for this example.

Listing 4-7. MultiFunction, Printable, and Fax

```
interface Printable {
  fun print(doc:String) = println("Printer:Printing $doc")
}
```

```
interface Fax {
  fun call(number: String) = println("Calling $number")
  fun print(doc: String) = println("Fax:Printing $doc")
  fun answer() = println("answering")
}

class MultiFunction : Printable, Fax {

  override fun print(doc:String)  {
    super<Fax>.print(doc)
    super<Printable>.print(doc)
    println("Multifunction: printing")
  }
}

fun main(args: Array<String>) {
  val mfc = MultiFunction()
  mfc.print("The quick brown fox")
  mfc.call("12345")
}
```

Classes

Another way to create a new type is to create a new class. A class is defined using (1) the *class* keyword, (2) an identifier, which will be its name, (3) an optional header, and (4) an optional body. Listing 4-8 shows a basic class.

Listing 4-8. A basic class in Kotlin

```
class Person() {
}
```

The header of the class is the pair of parentheses. Sometimes the header may contain parameters, but in the previous example, it doesn't have any. The pair of curly braces make up the class body. Technically, both the header and class body are optional, but most classes you'll encounter (and will write) might contain both header and body.

We can start using the class by creating objects out of it, like this

```
var person = Person()
```

If not for the noticeable absence of the *new* keyword, it looks a lot like how we would create objects in Java—Kotlin doesn't have a *new* keyword. The pair of parentheses after the type name (*Person*) is a call to a *no-arg* constructor. Let's go back to Listing 4-8 and look closer at the header portion of the class; this is one of the few areas where Kotlin looks and feels a bit different from Java. Java classes didn't have headers, but Kotlin does. This header is actually a constructor definition.

Constructors

Kotlin classes can have more than one constructor, which isn't very different from Java since Java classes can also have more than one constructor. However, Kotlin makes a distinction between a primary constructor and a secondary one. You will write a primary constructor on the header part of the class—like how we did it in Listing 4-9. If you write a secondary constructor, you will put it within the class body. Listing 4-9 shows a sample of a class with a primary constructor.

Listing 4-9. Person class with a primary constructor

```
class Person constructor(_name: String) { ❶
  var name:String   ❷
  init {            ❸
```

```
    name = _name    ❹
  }
}
```

---

❶   This is a primary constructor; because it's on the class header. This way of writing a constructor is essentially the same as in our example in Listing 4-8, except that Listing 4-8 doesn't contain the *constructor* keyword, while here (Listing 4-9), our constructor takes in a parameter.

❷   *name* is a member variable that will hold the value of the _name parameter.

❸   This is an *initializer* block similar to Java's *initializer*. This block runs before any object gets created. You can define more than one initializer block in your class; when that happens, *initializers* will be executed in the order they were defined in the class. An *initializer* block is a pair of curly braces prefixed by the keyword *init*. Initializers are typically used when there is only one constructor (the primary constructor)—because primary constructors cannot contain any code (whether statement or expressions).

❹   We can access arguments that were passed to the primary constructor from an initializer block.

When the primary constructor doesn't have (or need) annotations or modifiers, we can omit the *constructor* keyword like this

```
class Person (_name: String) {
  var name:String
  init {
    name = _name
  }
}
```

We can further simplify the code by joining the init block and declaration of the name variable in a statement like this

```
class Person (_name: String) {
  var name:String = _name
}
```

You may also define the constructors within the class' body (just like in Java); when you write them as such, they're called secondary constructors. Listing 4-10 shows us a sample.

Listing 4-10. Employee class, with secondary constructor

```
class Employee {
  var name:String
  constructor(_name: String) {
    name = _name
  }
}
```

Notice in Listing 4-10 that we didn't have to use the *init* block because we initialized the name variable within the constructor body. A secondary constructor, unlike a primary constructor, can contain code.

Listing 4-11. class Employee, with two secondary constructors

```
class Employee  {
  var name:String = ""      ❶
  var empid:String = ""

  constructor(_name: String) : this(_name, "1001")  ❷
  constructor(_name:String, _id: String) {          ❸
    name = _name
    empid = _id
  }
}
```

❶ We have to initialize our member variables because Kotlin won't be able to tell where we are doing the initialization.

❷ A secondary constructor needs to have the *constructor* keyword. This constructor doesn't have a body; it's okay to write it like that. Furthermore, this constructor invokes another constructor, one that accepts two arguments.

❸ Another secondary constructor is defined for the Employee class. This one takes in two parameters, a name, and an employee id.

You can overload constructors in Kotlin, as we did in Java, as seen in Listing 4-11. And also, as in Java, we can invoke other constructors using the *this* keyword. The *this* keyword in Kotlin is the same as in Java; it refers to an instance of yourself. No surprises there. Notice, though, how we used the *this* construct to delegate the call to another secondary constructor. You need to chain the *this* call to the constructor definition using a colon (see bullet number 2 of Listing 4-11).

While Kotlin allows us to do parametric polymorphism on constructors via overloading, this isn't idiomatic Kotlin because you can get the same results by using Kotlin's ability to provide default values for function parameters. See Listing 4-12 for a simplified version of the Employee class example.

Listing 4-12. Simplified Employee class

```
class Employee (_name:String, _empid:String = "1001")  {
  val name = _name
  val empid = _empid
}
```

The code above is more concise. Furthermore, moving the constructor parameters to the primary constructor allowed us to declare the member variables using *val* rather than *var*. Using immutable variables is the preferred technique in Kotlin because it reduces coding errors overall. You can't accidentally change a property's value if it's immutable in the first place.

There is no hard and fast rule about writing constructors. You can write classes that have both primary and secondary constructors or classes that have one without the other.

Inheritance

Kotlin is an object-oriented language; as such, it supports class-based inheritance. Listing 4-13 shows two classes, class Person and class Employee, which inherits from Person.

Listing 4-13. Person and Employee class

```
class Person {
}

class Employee : Person() {
}
```

Kotlin uses the colon symbol for class inheritance (also for implementing interfaces, as we've seen earlier). There's a slight problem in the preceding example—it won't compile because Kotlin classes are final by default, unlike Java classes, which are open (non-final). You cannot extend or inherit from final classes. To fix the code, we have to make the Person class "inheritable"; we can do that by using the *open* keyword (an inheritance modifier) in the Person class. Listing 4-14 shows the solution.

Listing 4-14. Person and Employee class

```kotlin
open class Person {
}

class Employee : Person() {
}
```

You might wonder why Kotlin makes classes final by default (a big departure from Java); this behavior is considered correct behavior and good practice. To paraphrase a quote from Joshua Bloch's Effective Java (Addison-Wesley, 2008)—*"design and document for inheritance, otherwise, prohibit it"*—it means all classes and methods you don't intend to extend ought to be final, to begin with. In Kotlin, this is the automatic behavior. Listing 4-15 shows the Person class again, but this time, it has the *open* modifier, which implies we can extend it.

The being "automatically final" behavior isn't just for classes. It applies to member functions as well. When a function doesn't have an explicit *open* modifier, it is *final*.

Listing 4-15. Method overriding

```kotlin
open class Person(_name:String) {
  val name = _name

  open fun talk() {  ❶
    println("${this.javaClass.simpleName} talking")
  }
}

class Employee(_name:String, _empid:String = "1001") :
Person(_name) {
  val empid = _empid
```

```
override fun talk() { ❷
  super.talk() ❸
  println("Hello")
}

override fun toString():String{  ❹
  return "name: $name | id: $empid"
}
}
```

---

❶   You need to explicitly say that functions are *open* so subtypes can override them.

❷   Subtypes need to use the *override* keyword to make the function polymorphic. If you're using IntelliJ, it's smart enough to prevent compilation if you don't use the *override* keyword in this situation.

❸   We can call the super behavior from here; this effectively calls the `talk()` function of the supertype (class *Person*).

❹   We're overriding the `toString()` function. This behavior was inherited from the *Person* class, which in turn, it inherited from class *Any*. You can think of class *Any* as Kotlin's equivalent for the *java.lang.Object*.

Remember that when you mark a function as *open*, it will remain open for overriding by its direct and indirect subtypes unless you mark the function as *final* again. To illustrate this point, let's see Listing 4-16.

Listing 4-16. class Person, Employee, and Programmer

```
open class Person(_name:String) {
  val name = _name

  open fun talk() { ❶
    println("${this.javaClass.simpleName} talking")
  }
}
```

```
open class Employee(_name:String, _empid:String = "1001") :
Person(_name) {
  val empid = _empid

    override fun talk() { ❷
     super.talk()
     println("Employee overriding talk()")
  }

  override fun toString():String{
    return "name: $name | id: $empid"
  }
}

class Programmer(_name:String) : Employee(_name) {
  override fun talk() { ❸
    super.talk()
    println("Programmer overriding talk()")
  }
}
```

---

❶ The talk() function is marked as *open* for the first time.

❷ We can override talk() in the Employee subtype.

❸ We can still override talk() in the Programmer subtype even if the Employee
   class did not mark the function as *open*. Function talk()implicitly stays open
   through the inheritance chain unless we mark it as *final* somewhere in the chain.

Listing 4-17 demonstrates how to make a function *closed* again in the
middle of the inheritance chain.

Listing 4-17. How to make a function final, again

```kotlin
open class Person(_name:String) {
  val name = _name

  open fun talk() {
    println("${this.javaClass.simpleName} talking")
  }
}

open class Employee(_name:String, _empid:String = "1001") :
Person(_name) {
  val empid = _empid

   final override fun talk() {
    super.talk()
    println("Employee overriding talk()")
  }

  final override fun toString():String{ ❶
    return "name: $name | id: $empid"
  }
}

class Programmer(_name:String) : Employee(_name) {
  override fun talk() { ❷
    super.talk()
    println("Programmer overriding talk()")
  }
}
```

❶   Seeing the *final* and *override* keywords on the same line seems odd, but it's
    perfectly legal. It means we are overriding the function and, at the same time,
    closing it for further inheritance. The *final* keyword in this function affects only
    subtypes of the Employee class, but not the Employee class itself.

❷   This statement won't compile anymore. The talk() function was marked *final*
    in the supertype (Employee class).

Properties

Properties are important for POJOs (Plain OldJava Objects). They're useful
for modeling domain objects. Typically (in Java), you create properties by
defining member variables—usually by following naming conventions—
and these variables are customarily prefixed by *get* and *set*. After that, you'll
create accessor methods to get and set the values of the member variables.
Listing 4-18 shows a typical POJO in Java with getter and setter methods.

Listing 4-18. Person class in Java with a single property

```
public class Person {
  private String name;

  public String getName() {
    return this.name;
  }
  public void setName(String name) {
    this.name = name
  }
}
```

```
public static void main(String []args) {
  Person person = new Person();
  person.setName("John Doe");
  System.out.println(person.getName());
  }
}
```

In the preceding example, we have class Person with just one property (*name*). We did this by making the *name* variable private so we can control the variable's state only via accessor methods. We had to do this kind of coding in Java because the language did not have native support for properties. We don't have to do this in Kotlin because it has language support for properties. Let's rewrite an equivalent of the previous POJO example in Kotlin (see Listing 4-19).

Listing 4-19. Person class with a single property

```
class Person(_name:String) { ❶
  val name:String = _name ❷
}

fun main(args: Array<String>) {
  var person = Person("John Smith")
  println(person.name) ❸
}
```

---

❶ A constructor takes in a parameter; this lets us set the name of the object at the time of object creation.

❷ We can access constructor parameters in the class body.

❸ This statement may look like we are directly accessing the name member variable, but we are not. This statement actually calls the get accessor method. Kotlin works in the background to provide automatic accessors and backing fields.

We can further simplify the Person example; Listing 4-20 shows us how.

Listing 4-20. Simplified Person class

```
class Person(val name:String)

fun main(args: Array<String>) {
  var person = Person("John Smith")
  println(person.name)
}
```

The code above is the most concise way of defining a property in Kotlin. It's also considered idiomatic. Notice the changes we made in the code.

- The parameter in the primary constructor now has a *val* declaration which makes the constructor parameter an immutable property. If you want to make a mutable (read/write) property, use the *var* keyword instead.

- We no longer need to differentiate the identifier in the constructor parameter with the member variable; hence we dropped the leading underscore in the _name variable.

- We can drop the entire class body since we no longer need it. The class body only contains the code to transfer the value of the constructor parameter to the member variable. Since Kotlin will automatically define a backing field for the constructor parameter, we don't have to do anything anymore in the class body.

The code in Listing 4-20 shows the most basic way to define data objects in Kotlin (Java programmers refer to them as POJOs or plain old java objects). We can automagically define properties with proper mutator methods by simply using either *val* or *var* in the primary constructor parameters. However, there will still be situations when you will need to exercise more control over the "getting" and "setting" process of these properties. Kotlin allows us to do that as well.

We can take over the automatic "getting" and "setting" process by doing the following:

1. Declare the property in the body of the class, not in the primary constructor

2. Provide getter and setter methods in the class body

The full syntax for declaring a property is as follows:

```
var <property name>:[<property type>][=<initializer>]
  [<getter>]
  [<setter>]
```

Listing 4-21 shows some basic usage of custom accessor methods.

Listing 4-21. Custom accessor methods

```
class Employee {
  var name: String = ""    ❶
    get() {  ❷
      Log("Getting name")  ❸
      return field  ❹
    }
    set(value) {  ❺
      Log("Setting value of name")
      field = value ❻
    }
}
```

```
fun Log(msg:String) {
  println(msg)
}

fun main(args: Array<String>) {
  var emp = Employee()
  emp.name = "John Doe"  ❼
  println(emp.name) ❽
}
```

---

❶   We declare and define the *property* inside the class body instead of capturing it as parameter in the primary constructor. We initialize it to an empty String first.

❷   The syntax for get() looks a lot like the syntax for defining a function, except we don't write the *fun* keyword before it.

❸   This part is where you write custom code. This statement will run every time someone tries to access the name property.

❹   The *field* keyword is a special one. It refers to the *backing field* Kotlin automatically provided when we defined the property called *name*. The name member variable isn't a simple variable, Kotlin makes an automatic *backing field* for it, but we don't have direct access to that variable. We can, however, access it via the *field* keyword, like what we did here.

❺   The value parameter corresponds to the data that the runtime will assign to the property when it creates the Employee object (see bullet number ❼ below).

❻   After we've performed our custom logic, we can now set the value of the field.

❼   This statement will trigger the set accessor logic. See bullet number ❺.

❽   This statement will trigger the get accessor logic. See bullet number ❷.

You might wonder why we used the *field* keyword in the *getter* and *setter* method. Why couldn't we just code the accessor methods like how we did it in Java? Let's explore this using Listing 4-22.

Listing 4-22. Wrong way to code getter and setter for properties

```
class Employee {
  var name: String = ""
    get() {
      Log("Getting lastname")
      return this.name          ❶
    }
    set(value) {
      Log("Setting value of lastname")
      this.name = value   ❷
    }
}
```

---

❶   This statement results in a recursive call, which will eventually throw
    StackOverflowError.

❷   So, will this.

In Listing 4-22, the expression this.name does not access the
member variable name. Instead, it calls the default accessor methods,
which Kotlin automatically provides when you define a property for the
class. So, calling this.name from within an accessor function will result
in a tailspin of recursive calls, and eventually, the runtime will throw a
StackOverflowError. To prevent the recursive problem, we use the *field*
keyword when referring to the backing field of a property name.

Data Classes

When working with data objects, we typically store them on collections like
ArrayList, HashMap, HashSet, etc. You might remember that in Java, we
needed to override the POJO's equals(), hashCode(), and toString()
methods, to make them work properly with Collections.

In the previous section, we've seen how easily we can create the analog of POJOs in Kotlin. We can simply define properties in our classes, and that'll be good to go. For simple use cases, the data objects we created earlier should be good enough. But you'll find that classes with properties aren't enough when you need to do things like store value objects in Collections or compare objects with one another for content equality. To utilize value objects properly from within Collection objects, we need to be able to compare objects with each other reliably. In Java, we use to solve this kind of problem by overriding some methods of the java.lang. Object, namely, the equals() and hashCode() methods. These methods are the key players when we're making object comparison. Consider the code sample in Listing 4-23.

Listing 4-23. Comparing two Employee objects

```kotlin
class Employee(val name:String)

fun main(args: Array<String>) {

  val e1 = Employee("John Doe")
  val e2 = Employee("John Doe")

  println(e1 == e2) // output is false
}
```

Remember that in Kotlin, the double equals operator actually invokes the equals() function of the operands being compared—and since everything in Kotlin is an object, they all have the equals() function since it's inherited from the supertype *Any*. If we let the Employee class stand as it does in Listing 4-23, it will use the implementation of the equals() function from class *Any*, and it doesn't know how to compare Employee objects. To resolve this, we can override the equals() method and provide an implementation on how to compare Employee objects.

> **Note**   Like Java, Kotlin follows a single-rooted class inheritance.
> If we don't specify a superclass in a class definition, the class will
> implicitly extend *Any*. This class is the supertype of all non-nullable
> types in Kotlin.

To fix the code in Listing 4-23, we can override the equals(), and
hashCode() functions as shown in Listing 4-24.

Listing 4-24. Overriding the hashCode() and equals() function

```
import java.util.*

class Employee(val name:String){
  override fun equals(obj:Any?):Boolean { ❶
    var retval = false
    if(obj is Employee) { ❷
      retval  = name == obj.name ❸
    }
    return retval
  }
  override fun hashCode(): Int { ❹
    return Objects.hash(name)
  }
}

fun main(args: Array<String>) {

  val e1 = Employee("John Doe")
  val e2 = Employee("John Doe")

  println(e1)              ❺
  println(e1 == e2)        ❻
}
```

❶   The equals() function in class *Any* is *open*. We can override it.

❷   We check first if we are comparing an *Employee* object to another *Employee* object. The *is* keyword performs two functions: (1) it checks if *obj* is an instance of *Employee*, and (2) it automatically casts *obj* to an *Employee* object

❸   The runtime automatically casts *obj* as an *Employee* object. The *is* keyword was responsible for that. We can now safely compare the name member variables of the two objects.

❹   We usually override the hashCode() function when we store the data object in Collections where the comparison of hash code is material, for example, *HashSet*, *HashMap*, etc. For our small example, it wasn't necessary. But typically, if you override the hashCode() function, you'll also override the equals() function.

❺   This statement calls the Employee object's toString() function; this function is found on the supertype *Any*. The default implementation of toString() gives us an output of something like this "Employee@ae805cc4".

❻   This statement prints "true".

This kind of coding practice is prevalent in Java, and for those reasons, quite a few IDEs have the capabilities to generate the boilerplate code of toString(), equals(), and hashCode(). While we can still do these things in Kotlin, we don't have to. The only thing we need to do in Kotlin is to make Employee a data class. Listing 4-25 shows us how.

Listing 4-25. Employee data class

```kotlin
data class Employee(val name:String) ❶

fun main(args: Array<String>) {
  val e1 = Employee("John Doe")
  val e2 = Employee("John Doe")
```

```
  println(e1)        ❷
  println(e1 == e2) ❸
}
```

---

❶ To make any class in Kotlin a *data class*, just use the keyword *data* on the class declaration.

❷ We get a bonus of a nicer toString() output with data classes. This one now prints "Employee(name=John Doe)".

❸ Also, the equals() comparison returns true.

Visibility Modifiers

Kotlin uses almost the same keywords as Java for controlling visibility. The keywords *public, private,* and *protected* mean the same in Kotlin as in Java. But, the default visibility is where the difference lies. In Kotlin, the default visibility is public whenever you omit the visibility modifier.

Listing 4-26 shows class Foo, where the class, its member functions, and variables do not have explicit visibility or access modifiers, which means the class and all its members are, by default, public access.

Listing 4-26. Class Foo

```
class Foo {
  var bar:String = ""
  fun doSomething() {

  }
}
```

To change the visibility to something less permissive, you must declare that explicitly. In contrast, Java's default visibility is *package-private,* meaning it's only available to classes on the same package. Kotlin doesn't have a *package-private* equivalent because Kotlin doesn't use packages to manage visibility. Packages in Kotlin are simply a way to organize files and prevent name clashes.

In place of Java's package-private, Kotlin introduces the *internal* keyword, which means visible in a *module*. A module is simply a collection of files; it can be (1) an IntelliJ module or project, (2) an Eclipse project, (3) a Maven project, or (4) a Gradle project. To demonstrate some of the visibility modifiers in action, see Listing 4-27.

Listing 4-27. Demonstrating visibility modifiers

```
internal open class Foo {  ❶
  private fun boo() = println("boo")
  protected fun doo() = println("doo")
}

fun Foo.bar() { ❷
  boo() ❸
  doo() ❹
}

fun main(args: Array<String>) {
  var fu = Foo()
  fu.bar()
}
```

❶ We marked class *Foo* as *internal*, which makes it visible only to classes and top-level functions that are within the same module and whose visibility is also marked *internal.*

❷ This is an error. We marked the *extension function* as *public*, but we marked the receiver of the function (Foo) as *internal*. Class *Foo* is less visible than the extension function; hence, the compiler prohibits it.

❸ Function boo() is private to the class; we can't reach it from here.

❹ Function doo() is protected; we can't reach it from here.

We need to fix the visibility errors to make Listing 4-27 run without problems. Listing 4-28 shows the solution.

Listing 4-28. class Foo, corrected visibility errors

```kotlin
internal open class Foo {
  internal fun boo() = println("boo")
  internal fun doo() = println("doo")
}

internal fun Foo.bar() {
  boo()
  doo()
}

fun main(args: Array<String>) {
  var fu = Foo()
  fu.bar()
}
```

Inheritance Modifiers

Kotlin's visibility modifiers are *final, open, abstract,* and *override.* They affect inheritance. We've used *final, open,* and *override* earlier in the chapter, so the only keyword we haven't used is *abstract.* The *abstract* keyword has the same meaning in Kotlin as in Java; it also applies to classes and functions.

When you mark a class as *abstract*, it becomes implicitly *open*, so you don't need to use the *open* modifier. It becomes redundant. Interfaces don't need to be declared *abstract* and *open* since they are implicitly, already, *abstract* and *open*.

Object Declarations

Java's *static* keyword did not make the cut in Kotlin's list of keywords. There is no *static* equivalent in Kotlin; in its place, Kotlin introduces the *object* and *companion* keywords.

The *object* keyword allows us to define both a class and its instance all at the same time. More specifically, it defines only a single instance of that class, which makes this keyword a good way to define *singletons* in Kotlin. Listing 4-29 shows the basic usage of the *object* keyword.

Listing 4-29. Using the object keyword to define a singleton

```
object Util {
  fun foo() = println("foo")
}

fun main(args: Array<String>) {
  Util.foo() // prints "foo"
}
```

We substitute the *object* keyword in place of the *class* keyword; this defines the class and creates a single instance of itself. To call the functions in this object, you need to prefix the dot (.) with the object's name, just like we would call static methods in Java.

Object declarations may contain most things you can write in class, like initializers, properties, functions, and member variables. A constructor is the only thing you cannot write inside an object declaration. That's because you don't need a constructor. The object declaration creates an instance already at the point of definition, so a constructor is unnecessary. Listing 4-30 shows some basic usage and definition for an object declaration.

Listing 4-30. Initializers, properties, functions, and member variables in object declarations

```
object Util {
  var name = ""
    set(value) {
      field = value
    }

  init {
    println("Initializing Util")
  }

  fun foo() = println(name)
}

fun main(args: Array<String>) {
  Util.name = "Bar"
  Util.foo() // prints "Bar"
}
```

Key Takeaways

- Kotlin interfaces are almost similar to that of Java, except that you can declare properties in interfaces, although they still are not allowed to have backing fields. Like Java, Kotlin interfaces can have *default* implementations.

- Kotlin classes are defined a bit differently than their Java counterparts. Classes are, by default, final and public.

- Kotlin has two kinds of constructors. You can define primary and secondary constructors. Primary constructors are a good way to create simple value objects. However, to create really useful value objects, Kotlin's data classes are a good way to go.

- Kotlin has almost the same mechanism for controlling visibility as Java, except that Kotlin replaced Java's *package-private* with the *internal* keyword.

CHAPTER 5

Higher Order Functions and Lambdas

We will revisit functions in this chapter, but a different kind. The kind that supports functional programming.

What we'll cover:

- Higher order functions

- Lambdas

- Closures

- With and apply

Higher Order Functions

Higher order functions operate on other functions by taking them in as parameters or returning them. The term higher order functions come from the world of Math, where there is a more formal distinction between functions and other values.

© Ted Hagos 2023
T. Hagos, *Beginning Kotlin*, https://doi.org/10.1007/978-1-4842-8698-2_5

Before discussing why we need higher order functions, let's attend to its mechanics first. Let's explore how to write them and what they look like. Let's see Listing 5-1, which shows a function that takes another function as a parameter.

Listing 5-1. A function that accepts another function

```
fun executor(action:() -> Unit) {
  action()
}
```

In the preceding code sample, *action* is the parameter's name, and its type is written as ()-> Unit, which signifies that its type is *function*. We wrote the *function type* with a pair of parentheses, followed by the arrow operator (a dash plus the greater than sign), followed by a type which the function is expected to return. In Listing 5-1, the function parameter doesn't return anything; hence it's declared as *Unit*.

This way of writing code may look unusual, particularly if you haven't used a language where functions are treated the same way variables are treated. In Kotlin, functions are first-class citizens. We can pass (or return) functions from anywhere we can pass (or return) variables. Wherever you can use a variable, you can also use a function.

Let's go back to Listing 5-1. If we want to change the type of the *action* parameter to String, we can write something like the following (Listing 5-2).

Listing 5-2. If action was of type String

```
fun executor(action:String) {
  action()
}
```

But that's not the case. We want *action* to be of type *function*. In Kotlin, a function isn't just a named collection of statements; it's also a type. So, just like *String, Int,* or *Float,* we can declare a variable to be of type *function.* A function type has three components: (1) the parenthesized parameter type list, (2) the arrow operator, and (3) the return type.

In Listing 5-1, the parenthesized parameter type list is empty, but it won't always be the case. It's empty right now because the function we intend to pass to executor() doesn't accept any parameters. The return type of executor() is Unit because the function we intend to pass to it doesn't return any value—that also will not always be the case; you may want to return an Int or String sometimes.

Next, let's see how to declare and define a variable to be of *function* type. Listing 5-3 shows an example.

Listing 5-3. How to declare and define a function type

```
val doThis:() -> Unit  = {
  println("action")
}
```

The LHS (left-hand side) doesn't require much explanation, we're just declaring a variable named *doThis* to be of *type function,* and the function doesn't return anything (hence, the Unit return type). The RHS (right-hand side) looks like a function without a header—there is no *fun* keyword, and there's also no function name—this is a lambda. Think of lambdas as anonymous functions. We'll get to lambdas in the next section.

The next code sample (Listing 5-4) shows how to use higher order functions.

Listing 5-4. Complete code for doThis and executor() examples

```
val doThis:() -> Unit  = { ❶
  println("action")
}
```

```
fun executor(action:() -> Unit) { ❷
  action() ❸
  action.invoke() ❹
}

fun main(args: Array<String>) {
  executor(doThis) ❺
}
```

---

❶ *doThis* is a variable declared and defined as a *function type* with a lambda expression on the right-hand side.

❷ executor() is a function that accepts another function as a parameter named *action* whose type is *function* and is written as () ➤ Unit (because *action* doesn't return anything).

❸ By appending a pair of parentheses on the name of the parameter (action), we can call it like a function.

❹ This statement shows us another way of invoking the *action* function, but calling it as action() is more idiomatic and hence, preferred.

❺ Inside the main function, we call executor(), and we pass *doThis*. Note that we're not passing doThis() with the parentheses. We don't want to invoke *doThis* and then pass the resulting value to executor(). We want to pass *doThis* not as a resultant value but as a function definition. The idea is to invoke *doThis* within the body of the executor() function.

In Listing 5-4, we wrote *doThis* as a property whose value is a lambda, this is fine, but it might not feel like a natural way to write functions. Another way to write Listing 5-4 is shown as follows (Listing 5-5).

Listing 5-5. Another way of writing the doThis and executor() examples

```
fun doThis() { ❶
  println ("action")
}

fun executor(action:() -> Unit) {
  action()
}

fun main(args: Array<String>) {
  executor(::doThis) ❷
}
```

❶ doThis is now defined in the usual way that we write functions, with the *fun* keyword and the function name in the header.

❷ We call ::doThis with a double colon, which means we are resolving the function within the current *package.*

Lambda and Anonymous Functions

Lambdas and anonymous functions are called *function literals.* These are functions that are not declared and are usually passed immediately as an expression (typically as an argument to higher order functions)—this is why they don't need a name.

We've seen lambda expressions earlier in Listing 5-3, where we defined a property called *doThis* (whose type is a function). But that was a verbose way of working with a function type. We usually don't need to explicitly declare the function's return type because Kotlin has type inference. Let's see how this works in Listing 5-6.

Listing 5-6. Concise version of Listing 5-3

val *doThis* = {

```
    println("action")
```
}

As you've seen earlier, the preceding example is typically passed as an argument to a higher order function. Still, it's perfectly alright to call this function from elsewhere (like function main or any top-level function) like this

```
doThis()
```

or something like this

```
doThis.invoke()
```

The first one feels more natural; it's also considered more idiomatic, but lambda expressions aren't meant to be used like that. Lambda expressions shine when used within the context of higher order functions.

Using the full syntactic form of the lambda expression—as we did in Listing 5-5—is quite okay, but lambda expressions in the wild don't usually look like that. In Listing 5-7, we rewrite the code in Listing 5-5; but this time, instead of declaring and defining a named lambda, we will pass it as an argument to a higher order function (*executor*).

Listing 5-7. Pass a lambda to a higher order function

```
fun main(args: Array<String>) {
  executor(
    { println("do this") } ❶
  )
}
```

```
fun executor(action:() -> Unit) {
  action()
}
```

  This block is the function literal. We are passing the lambda expression itself directly to the higher order function. A lambda expression is enclosed in a pair of curly braces—just like the body of a function.

Parameters in Lambda Expressions

Listing 5-8 shows a typical Kotlin function.

Listing 5-8. Simple function to display a String

```
fun display(msg:String) {
  println("Hello $msg")
}
```

To rewrite the preceding code sample as a lambda, it looks like Listing 5-9.

Listing 5-9. Display function written as lambda

```
{ msg:String -> println("Hello $msg") }
```

Notice the entire function header? The keyword *fun* and the function name are completely gone, and we put the parameter list inside the lambda expression. The whole expression is enclosed in curly braces.

In a lambda expression, we write the parameter list on the arrow operator's left-hand side, and the function's body is on the right. You will also notice that the parameters in a lambda expression don't need to be inside the parentheses because the arrow operator separates the parameter list from the lambda body. You can also omit the type declaration of String in the parameter, like Listing 5-10.

Listing 5-10. Omitted type declaration in the parameter list

```
{ msg -> println("Hello $msg") }
```

In cases where the lambda expression takes only one parameter (like the preceding sample), we can omit the parameter declaration and the arrow operator. We can rewrite the code in Listing 5-10 even more concisely, like Listing 5-11.

Listing 5-11. The implicit it

```
{ println("Hello $it") }
```

Kotlin generates the *it* parameter name if the context expects a lambda with only one parameter, and its type can be inferred. Listing 5-12 shows the full code for declaring and using a lambda expression within the context of a higher order function. Now we have the *functional programming* version of the Hello World example.

Listing 5-12. Full code for the lambda example

```
fun main(args: Array<String>) {
  executor({ println("Hello $it") })
}

fun executor(display:(msg:String) -> Unit) {
  display("World")
}
```

Writing and using lambdas with more than one parameter is not much different from our single parameter example, as long as you write the parameter list on the left side of the arrow operator. Listing 5-13 shows an example.

Listing 5-13. Lambdas with more than one parameter

```
fun main(args: Array<String>) {
  doer({ x,y -> println(x + y) })
}

fun doer(sum:(x:Int,y:Int) -> Unit) {
  sum(1,2)
}
```

There may be times when a higher order function needs to take mixed types (function types and other types like String, Int, etc.). We can write that function like Listing 5-14.

Listing 5-14. Higher order function with other parameters

```
fun executor(arg: String = "Mondo", display:(msg:String)
-> Unit) {
  display(arg)
}
```

We can call this function like this

```
executor("Earth", {println("Hola $it")})
```

And since *executor's* first parameter has a default value, we can still invoke it like this

```
executor({println("Hola $it")})
```

Kotlin allows us to be precise in our syntax with lambdas. In cases where the lambda is expected as the last parameter in a higher order function, we can write the lambda outside the parentheses of the invoking function, like this

```
executor() { println("Hello $it")}
```

117

And if the lambda is the only parameter, we can even omit the parentheses entirely, like this one

```
executor { println("Hello $it")}
```

The simplification may not seem like a big deal right now, but you might appreciate the syntactical improvements later on as you write more and more lambda expressions. The Kotlin Standard library makes heavy use of these shorthands.

Closures

When you use lambda expressions inside a function, the lambda can access the function's *closure*. The closure comprises the local variables in the outer scope and all the parameters of the enclosing function. Listing 5-15 explores an example.

Listing 5-15. Lambda accessing its closure

```
fun main(args: Array<String>) {
  executor(listOf(1..1000).flatten()) ❶
}

fun executor(numbers:List<Int>) {
 var sum = 0;
 numbers.forEach {        ❷
   if ( it % 2 == 0 ) {
     sum += it            ❸
   }
 }
  println("Sum of all even numbers = $sum")
}
```

❶   We're passing a list of *Ints* to the executor() function. Using the *rangeTo* function in operator form (..) is a handy way to generate a list of integers from 1 up to 1000. But you'd have to use the flatten() function to make it a list of *Ints*.

❷   *forEach* is a higher order function; it takes a lambda that lets us walk through the items in the list. The forEach only has one parameter, and we can access that parameter using the implicit *it* parameter name.

❸   The *sum* local variable is part of the *closure* within the function body where the lambda is defined. Lambdas have access to their *closures.*

Note   In Java lambdas, you can only access variables in its closure if that same variable is final; Kotlin does not have this restriction.

with and apply

Kotlin uses lambdas heavily. You will find quite a number of lambdas all over Kotlin's built-in library.

Two built-in functions in Kotlins standard library (*Standard.kt*) are *with* and *apply*. These functions showcase Kotlin's lambda capabilities and what makes them stand from their Java counterparts. Kotlin lambdas can call methods of a different object without additional qualifiers in the lambda body—these are called *lambdas with receivers.*

The functions *with* and *apply* are interesting not because they let us do multiple operations on the same object without repeating its name (which is handy). They're interesting because they appear like they were baked into the language (which they're not). They simply are functions that were made special by *extension functions* and *lambdas.*

Listing 5-16 shows a simple class and how to set some of its properties. The creation of an *Event* instance and the setting of its various properties are happening inside *function main*. Notice that for every property we set, we have to explicitly resolve the property back to the object reference—and this might be just fine. After all, this was how we coded in Java. This chore is, sort of, expected.

Listing 5-16. class Event

```
import java.util.Date

data class Event(val title:String) {
  var date = Date()
  var time = ""
  var attendees = mutableListOf<String>()

  fun create() {
    print(this)
  }
}

fun main(args: Array<String>) {

  val mtg = Event("Management meeting")

  mtg.date = Date(2018,1,1)
  mtg.time = "0900H"
  mtg.attendees.add("Ted")

  mtg.create()
}
```

If we use the *with* function to refactor the code, it will look like Listing 5-17.

Listing 5-17. Using the with function

```
fun main(args: Array<String>) {

  val mtg = Event("Management meeting")

  with(mtg) {
    date = Date(2018,1,1)
    time = "0900H"
    attendees.add("Ted")

  }
}
```

The *with* function takes an object (*mtg*) and a lambda. Inside the lambda, we can work with the *mtg* object without the need to explicitly reference it. We can do such things because the *mtg* object is a *receiver* of the lambda—remember the extension functions in Chapter 3, "Functions"? And because *mtg* is the receiver inside the lambda, the *this* keyword points to the *mtg* object. We could have referenced *this* explicitly, but that wouldn't be any better. By omitting the explicit reference to *this*, the resulting code is cleaner. Also, the convention to put the lambda outside the parentheses works here because it makes the construct look as if *with* is built into the language.

The *apply* function can do the same thing; it's very similar to the *with* function except that it returns the receiver (the object passed to it)—the *with* function doesn't. Listing 5-18 shows how to use the *apply* function.

Listing 5-18. Using the apply function

```
fun main(args: Array<String>) {

  val mtg = Event("Management meeting")

  mtg.apply {                    ❶
    date = Date()                ❷
```

```
    time = "0900H"
    attendees.add("Ted")
  }.create()              ❸
}
```

---

❶ apply is an extension function and the *mtg* object becomes its *receiver.*

❷ And because the *mtg* object is the *receiver*, *this* refers to the *mtg* object.

❸ When the lambda returns, it returns the *receiver*, which is a *mtg* object; hence, we can chain some calls into it.

There are many more functions in *Standard.Kt* like *run, let, also,* etc., but these two examples using *with* and *apply* should give us an idea of what lambdas are capable of.

Key Takeaways

- Kotlin functions are more than just a named collection of statements. Function is also a type. You can use a *function type* anywhere you can use other types (like Int, String, etc.)—functions are first-class citizens in Kotlin.

- Lambdas and anonymous functions are function literals. They're like regular functions, but they don't have a name. You can pass them around (to other functions) immediately as an expression.

- Kotlin lambdas can mutate variables in its closure.

- Higher order functions are functions that operate on other functions. They can accept function types as parameters or return function types.

CHAPTER 6

Collections

Knowledge of collections will let you solve tricky data structure problems
with ease. You don't need to write your own algorithm to handle sets,
maps, and lists. The collections API will do that for you; and that's what
we'll discuss in this chapter.

What we'll cover:

- Arrays

- Collections

- Filter and map

One of the real-world analogies for collections would be a purse or
a pouch filled with various things such as coins. The coins would be the
items and the pouch itself is the *collection*. So, based on this analogy, we
can say that a collection is a *container* of sorts that may have zero, one, or
many items in it. You might remember that we already have something
like that—an array. The array fits this description exactly because it can
contain zero or one or many items inside it. If this is the case, do we really
need to learn about other containers? In this chapter, we'll take a look at
arrays, collections, and some of the functions within the Kotlin collections
framework.

© Ted Hagos 2023
T. Hagos, *Beginning Kotlin*, https://doi.org/10.1007/978-1-4842-8698-2_6

Arrays

Coming from Java, you'll need to step back a bit before working with Kotlin arrays. In Java, these are special types, they have first-class support on the language level. In Kotlin, arrays are just types; more specifically, they are parameterized types. If you wanted to create an array of Strings, you might think that the following snippet might work:

```
var arr = {"1", "2", "3", "4" , "5"}
```

This code wouldn't make sense to Kotlin, it doesn't treat arrays as a special type. If we wanted to create an array of Strings like the example above, we can do it in a couple of ways. Kotlin has some library functions like *arrayOf, emptyArray*, and *arrayOfNulls* that we can use to facilitate array creation. Listing 6-1 shows how to create and populate an array using the *emptyArray* function.

Listing 6-1. Using the emptyArray function

```
var arr = emptyArray<String>();
arr += "1"
arr += "2"
arr += "3"
arr += "4"
arr += "5"
```

Adding elements to a Kotlin array isn't as verbose as it is in Java, but don't be fooled by nice syntax. Arrays are still fixed-size at the time of creation, even in Kotlin. Adding an element to an array is done by creating a new array that is bigger than the old array and then copying the elements of the old array into the new one. So, you see, it's still an expensive operation—even if we have a nice sugary syntax. Listing 6-2 shows how to use the *arrayOfNulls* function to do the same thing.

Listing 6-2. Using the arrayOfNulls function

```
var arr2 = arrayOfNulls<String>(2)
arr2.set(0, "1")
arr2.set(1, "2")
```

The integer argument of the arrayOfNulls function is the size of the array to be created. Unlike the empty array in Listing 6-1, this function gives you a chance to provide a size for the array you're about to create. By the way, you can still use bracket syntax for Kotlin arrays, the *get* and *set* methods of *Arrays* are just convenience functions. Listing 6-3 shows the use of the bracket syntax together with the new *get* and *set* functions.

Listing 6-3. get and set methods of Array

```
var arr2 = arrayOfNulls<String>(2)

// arr2.set(0, "1")
// arr2.set(1, "2")

arr2[0] = "1"
arr2[1] = "2"
println(arr2[0]) // same as arr2.get(0)
println(arr2[1])
```

Another way to create an array is using the *arrayOf* function. Listing 6-4 shows the snippet.

Listing 6-4. Using the arrayOf function

```
var arr4 = arrayOf("1", "2", "3")
```

This function is probably the closest syntax we can get to the Java array literal, which is probably why it is used by programmers more commonly. You can pass a comma-separated list of values to the function and that automatically populates the newly created array.

Lastly, arrays can be created using the Array constructor. The constructor takes in two arguments, the first of which is the size of the array to be created and the second argument is a lambda function that can return an initial value of each element.

Listing 6-5. Using the Array constructor

```
var arr5= Array<String>(5, {it.toString()})
```

In most situations when you need to work with arrays of numbers, using the *Array* class should suffice. You need to remember however that Array<Int>, for example, represents the ints as Integer objects rather than integer primitives. So, if you need to squeeze a bit more performance juice out of your code and really use the primitive number types, you can use the specialized array types of Kotlin.

The specialized classes like *ByteArray, IntArray, ShortArray,* and *LongArray* represent arrays of primitive types (like the ones in Java). These types let you work with arrays without the boxing and unboxing overhead of *Arrays* that uses the object counterparts of the number primitives. These specialized types actually do not inherit from *Array*, but they have the same sets of method and properties. Also, they have specialized factory functions that make them easier to work with. See Listing 6-6 for an example.

Listing 6-6. Special array types

```
var z = intArrayOf(1,2,3)
var y = longArrayOf(1,2,3)
var x = byteArrayOf(1,2,3)
var w = shortArrayOf(1,2,3)

println(Arrays.toString(z))
println(Arrays.toString(y))
```

```
println(Arrays.toString(x))
println(Arrays.toString(w))
```

I used the Arrays.toString() function so that we'll get a human-readable output when printing the contents. If you simply print the array without the helper function, it looks gibberish, like this

```
println(z) // outputs [Ljava.lang.String;@6ad5c04e
```

You can traverse arrays in a couple of ways. Firstly, you can use the trustworthy *for* loop, as shown in Listing 6-7.

Listing 6-7. Using a for loop to process each array element

```
for (i in z) {
  println("$i zee")
}
```

Or you could use the *forEach* function, like so

```
y.forEach { i -> println("$i why") }
```

If you need to keep track of both the index and the element of the array, you can use the *forEachIndexed* function, as shown in Listing 6-8.

Listing 6-8. Using the forEachIndexed function to traverse the array

```
x.forEachIndexed { index, element ->
  println("$index : $element")
}
```

Before we leave the subject of arrays, we need to remember that if you don't want any duplication on the contents of the array, you'll have to write that program logic yourself. Uniqueness of contents is not something that arrays will guarantee.

While arrays are very useful in many situations, they do have limitations, as you've seen in the previous discussions. Adding new elements to arrays, while the syntax is friendly, is still an expensive operation. You can't print them out without the use of helper functions (although this is not a big deal). Lastly, it doesn't have a facility for constraining the elements, for example, enforcing uniqueness. For some situations, these limitations may not be a big deal, but for others, these may be deal-killers. So, when we come up to the limitations of the arrays, we are coming up on the territory of Collections—they help us deal with such limitations.

The availability of the collections framework as part of the development kit may not be such a big deal for you. After all, you came from Java and it has an impressive collections framework. But you need to remember that before languages like Java, C#, Python, etc., there were no collections frameworks. Programmers had to write their own program logic in order to deal with problems like resizable arrays, last in first out access, hash tables or hash maps, etc. These aren't simple storage issues, but rather, they are data structure issues. It's quite difficult to implement these data structure logic on your own, there are a lot of edge cases to get right. Although there might still be legitimate reasons to implement your own data structures, probably for performance reasons, in most cases, you'd be better off to use the built-in collections framework.

Collections

The Kotlin collections are actually direct instances of the collections in the JDK. There's no conversion of wrapping involved. So, if you didn't skimp on your study of collections while you were in Java, that will certainly come in handy now. Although Kotlin didn't define its own collections code, it did add quite a few convenience functions to the framework, which is a welcome addition because it makes the collections easier to work with.

Before we go to the code examples and more details, something needs to be said why it is called a collections framework. The reason it's called a framework is because the data structures are very diverse, in and of themselves. Some of them put constraints on how we go through the collection, they impose certain order of traversal. Some of the collections constrain the uniqueness of the data elements, they won't allow you to put duplicates. And some of them let us work with the collections in pairs, like in a dictionary entry, you'll have a key with a corresponding value.

Figure 6-1 shows the hierarchy of the Kotlin collections framework. At the top of the hierarchy are the interfaces *Iterable* and *MutableIterable*, they are the parents of all the collection classes we will work with. As you may have noticed in the diagram, each Java collection has two representations in Kotlin: a read-only one and a mutable one. The mutable interfaces map directly to the Java interfaces while the immutable interfaces lack all of the mutator methods of their mutable counterparts.

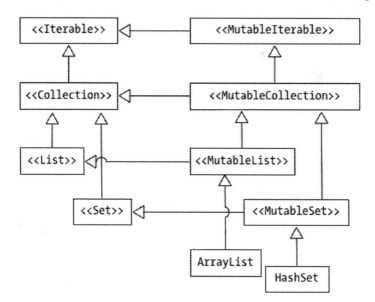

Figure 6-1. *Collections framework*

Kotlin doesn't have a dedicated syntax for creating lists or sets, but it does provide us with library functions to facilitate creation. Table 6-1 lists some of them.

Table 6-1. *Kotlin collections and their creation functions*

Collection	Read only	Mutable .
list	listOf	mutableListOf, arrayListOf
set	setOf	mutableSetOf, hashSetOf, linkedSetOf, sortedSetOf
map	mapOf	mutableMapOf, hashMapOf, linkedMapOf, sortedMapOf

Note   Although the map class doesn't inherit from either *Iterable* or *MutableIterable* (Figure 6-1), it's still represented in Kotlin as two distinct versions, a mutable and an immutable one.

Lists

A list is a type of collection that has a specific iteration order. It means that if we added a couple of elements to the list, and then we step through it, the elements would come out in a very specific order—it's the order by which they were added or inserted. They won't come out in a random order or reverse chronology, but precisely in the sequence they were added. It implies that each element in the list has a placement order, an index number that indicates its ordinal position. The first element to be added will have its index at 0, the second will be 1, the third will be 2, and so on and so forth. So, just like an array, it is zero-based. Listing 6-9 shows the basic usage for a list.

Listing 6-9. Basic usage of lists

```kotlin
fun main(args: Array<String>) {

    val fruits = mutableListOf<String>("Apple")  ❶
    fruits.add("Orange")        ❷
    fruits.add(1, "Banana")     ❸
    fruits.add("Guava")

    println(fruits)  // prints [Apple, Banana, Orange, Guava]

    fruits.remove("Guava")      ❹
    fruits.removeAt(2)          ❺

    println(fruits.first() == "Strawberries") ❻
    println(fruits.last() == "Banana")        ❼

    println(fruits) //  prints [Apple, Banana]
}
```

---

❶   Creates a mutable list, the constructor function allows us to pass a variable argument which will be used to populate the list. In this case, we only passed one argument—we could have passed more.

❷   Adds an element to the list, "Orange" will come right after "Apple" since we did not specify the ordinal position for the insertion.

❸   Adds another element to the list, but this time, we told it where exactly to put the element. This one bumps down the "Orange" element and then inserts itself. Naturally, the ordinal position or the index of all the elements that come after it will change.

❹   You can remove elements by name. When an element is removed, the element next to it will take its place. The ordinal position of all the elements that comes after it will change accordingly.

❺   You can also remove elements by specifying its position on the list.

❻   You can ask if the first() element is equal to "Strawberries".

❼   You can also test if the last() element is equal to "Banana".

Sets

Sets are very similar to lists, both in operation and in structure, so, all of the things we've learned about lists apply to sets as well. Sets differ from lists in the way it puts constraints on the uniqueness of elements. It doesn't allow duplicate elements or the same elements within a set. It may seem obvious to many what the "same" means, but Kotlin, like Java, has a specific meaning for "sameness". When we say that two objects are the same, it means that we've subjected the objects to a test for structural equality. Both Java and Kotlin define a method called equals() which allows us to determine equivalence relationships between objects. This is generally what we mean by "sameness". Listing 6-10 shows some basic operations with sets.

Listing 6-10. Basic usage for sets

```
val nums = mutableSetOf("one", "two")  ❶
nums.add("two")                         ❷
nums.add("two")                         ❸
nums.add("three")                       ❹

println(nums) // prints [one, two, three]

val numbers = (1..1000).toMutableSet() ❺
numbers.add(6)
numbers.removeIf { i -> i % 2 == 0 }    ❻

println(numbers)
```

❶   Creates a mutable set and initializes it by passing a variable argument to the creator function.

❷   This doesn't do anything. It won't add "two" to the set because the element "two" is already in the set.

❸   No matter how many times you try to add "two", the set will reject it because it already exists.

❹   This, on the other hand, will be added because "three" doesn't exist in the elements yet.

❺   Creates a mutable set from a range. This is a handy way of creating a set (or a list) with many numeric elements.

❻   This demonstrates how to use a lambda to remove all the even numbers in the set.

Maps

Unlike lists or sets, maps aren't a collection of individual values, but rather, they are a collection of pairs of values. Think of a map like a dictionary or a phone book, its contents are organized using a key-value pair. For each key in a map, there is one and only one corresponding value. In a dictionary example, the key would be the *term*, and its value would be the *meaning* or the *definition* of the term.

The keys in a map are unique. Like sets, maps do not allow duplicate keys. However, the values in a map are not subjected to the same uniqueness constraints; two or more pairs in map may have the same value. Listing 6-11 shows some basic usage for maps.

Listing 6-11. Basic operations on a map

```
val dict = hashMapOf("foo" to 1)  ❶
dict["bar"] = 2                    ❷

val snapshot: MutableMap<String, Int> = dict ❸
snapshot["baz"] = 3                          ❹

println(snapshot)                  ❺
println(dict)                      ❻
println(snapshot["bar"]) // prints 2   ❼
```

---

❶ Creates a mutable map.

❷ Adds a new key and value to the map.

❸ Assigns the dict map to a new variable. This doesn't create a new map. It only adds an object reference to the existing map.

❹ Adds another key-value pair to the map.

❺ Prints {bar = 2, baz = 3, foo=1}.

❻ Also prints {bar = 2, baz = 3, foo=1}, because both snapshot and dict points to the same map.

❼ Gets the value from the map using the key.

Now that we've seen some examples of basic usage of collections, you probably have noticed that they share some common characteristics, maybe not 100% so with the map, but the list and the set have quite a lot of overlap. One good thing about working with the collections framework is the uniformity or regularity of certain operations throughout the entire collection. The skills and knowledge that we learn from working with lists, for example, commutes or translates nicely across sets and maps as well. Because of this, it's a good idea to be familiar with the collections protocol. Table 6-2 lists some of the more common operations on collections.

Table 6-2. *Common operations on collections*

Function or property	Description
size()	Tells you how many elements are in the collection. Works with lists, sets and maps
isEmpty()	Returns True if the collection is empty, False if it's not. Works with lists, sets, and maps
contains(arg)	Returns True if arg is within the collection. Works with lists, sets and maps
add(arg)	Add arg to the collection. This function returns true if arg was added—in the case of a list, arg will always be added. In the case of a set, arg will be added and return true the first time, but if the same arg is added the second time, it will return False. This member function is not found on maps
remove(arg)	Returns True if arg was removed from the collection, returns False is the collection is unmodified
iterator()	Returns an iterator over the elements of the object. This was inherited from the Iterable interface. Works with lists, sets, and maps

Collections Traversal

By now, we already know how to work with basic collections. We know how to create them, add and remove items from them. Another skill we will need to work effectively with collections is the ability to loop through them or traverse them. To do that, let's go back to Figure 6-1 and recall the inheritance structure of the collections framework.

In Figure 6-1, you'll notice that *Collections* inherits the *Iterable* interface. An *iterable* defines something that can be iterated over or stepped over. When a class inherits an Iterable interface, whether directly or indirectly, it means we can pull an iterator out of it and step through its elements one by one. And in each step, we can also pull the value of each element—it's up to your program logic what you want to do with those values, you can transform them, use it in an arithmetic operation or persist it in a storage, for example.

We can use a variety of ways to step through the elements in a collection. We can use the trusty *while* and *for* loops, if you prefer, but using the more modern *forEach* is more idiomatic—and a bit in vogue. Listing 6-12 shows how to step through a list using *while* and *for* loops.

Listing 6-12. Using while and for loops for collections

```
val basket = listOf("apple", "banana", "orange")
var iter = basket.iterator()
while (iter.hasNext()) {
  println(iter.next())
}

for (i in basket) {
  println(i)
}
```

Listing 6-12 is probably something close to how you worked with collections in Java, so it should look familiar. Listing 6-13 shows the equivalent codes when using the *forEach* function.

Listing 6-13. Using forEach

```
fruits.forEach { println(it) } ❶
nums.forEach { println(it) }   ❷

// for maps

dict.forEach { println(it) }   ❸
dict.forEach { t, u -> println("$t | $u") } ❹
```

❶ The lambda expression of the forEach has an implicit it parameter. The it parameter is the value of the current element. What this statement means is, for each item in *fruits*, do what's inside the lambda; which is in our case is just println().

❷ Same thing works for *sets.*

❸ Same thing works for *maps.*

❹ This is a variation of bullet no. 3 above, but this one allows us to work with the *key* and *value* separately.

Filter and Map

Filter and map are part of the essential skills you need to master in order to work with collections efficiently. Filtering allows us to work with the elements of a collection selectively. It narrows down the field. It basically returns a subset of the original collection. A map on the other hand allows us to transform either the elements or the collection itself.

Let's say, for example, that we have a list of numbers—integers to be precise, like this

```
val ints = (1..100).toList()
```

The variable *ints* contains a list of integers from 1 up until 100, in increments of one. If we wanted to work with only the even numbers in this list, we could do so by (1) creating a new list then (2) by iterating over the ints list and performing a modulo check for even numbers, and then (3) if the current element being processed is an even number, we add it to the new list. That code might look like Listing 6-14.

Listing 6-14. Using a for loop to sieve out the even numbers

```
val evenInts2 = mutableListOf<Int>()
for (i in ints) {
  if (i % 2 == 0) {
    evenInts2.add(i)
  }
}
```

Listing 6-14 is what might be called the "imperative" way of filtering out things. Nothing wrong with it, it's a little verbose, that's all. But it's perfectly readable, even by someone just starting out in programming. However, in Kotlin, the more idiomatic way of narrowing down collections is by using the *filter* function. If we were to do this using filters, it would be like this

```
val evenInts = ints.filter { it % 2 == 0 }
```

I did not even put a Listing label on it anymore because it's unnecessary, it's just one line. The filter function is a standard function in the collections library. You already know that the expression in the curly braces is a lambda. However, for filters, the more apt term is a lambda predicate. A lambda predicate is also a function literal, but the expression inside has to yield a Boolean value.

Going back to our example, the filter is invoked against a collection, a list of ints, for example. The result of filter operation is a smaller list or a subset. The list is trimmed down by iterating over each element and testing them against the condition specified in the lambda predicate. Any item that passes the test of the predicate will be included in the resulting subset.

Let's continue our example and work with our smaller list of even integers. Let's say that what we want now is to square each element in our list of even integers. This requires us to manipulate and transform each element in the list, and then return a new list that contains the transformed elements. If we were to solve this using a for loop, it would look like Listing 6-15.

Listing 6-15. Generate a list of squared ints using a for loop

```
val squaredInts2 = mutableListOf<Int>()
for (i in evenInts2) {
  squaredInts2.add( i * i )
}
println(squaredInts2)
```

Or we could have solved it using the *forEach* function in Collections. It would have looked like Listing 6-16.

Listing 6-16. Generate a list of squared ints using forEach

```
val squaredInts2 = mutableListOf<Int>()
evenInts2.forEach { squaredInts2.add(it * it) }
```

This is actually looking much better but transforming elements in a collection is really the province of the map function. So, let's solve the squared integers problem using maps. Listing 6-17 shows the code.

Listing 6-17. Using the map function

```
val squaredInts = evenInts.map { it * it}
println("Sum of squares of even nos <= 100 is ${squaredInts.
sum()}")
```

The only relevant statement in Listing 6-17 is the first one. The second statement just prints out the sum of all the even numbers from 1 up to 100. Also, the second line showcases another built-in function in the collections framework, the sum() function. It's pretty obvious what it does, it sums up the values in the collection.

Key Takeaways

- When working with a group of values, we can use either arrays or collections. Use arrays for simple data structures, but when you need to dynamically size your group of data or you need to put more constraints to it, like, a uniqueness constraint, you might be better served by collections.

- Arrays in Kotlin are unlike the ones in Java, they don't enjoy special treatment. In Kotlin, arrays are just classes.

- Kotlin provides specialized classes for arrays, if you feel you need to work with arrays without the overhead of boxing and unboxing.

- Kotlin collections are very similar to Java collections, but each of the Java collection classes is represented in two ways: a mutable and an immutable one.

- Kotlin collections have built-in functions like filter, map, and sum which make working with collections a bit easier.

CHAPTER 7

Generics

For the most part, Kotlin generics work the same way as Java generics; but they have some differences. In this chapter, we'll look at how to work with generics and how similar (or different) Kotlin's generics is with that of Java's.

What we'll cover:

- Using generics
- Constraints
- Variance
- Reified generics

Why Generics

Generics came to Java around 2004, when JDK 1.5 was released. Before generics, you could write codes like Listing 7-1.

Listing 7-1. Using a raw List, Java

```
List v = new ArrayList();
v.add("test");
Integer i = (Integer) v.get(0); // Run time error
```

Why would you do such a careless thing? You might ask. You can see from Listing 7-1 that we put a String in the ArrayList; so, just don't do any operation that's not appropriate for a String; problem solved. It may not always be as easy as that. The sample code is contrived and it's easy to spot the error right now, but if you're doing something non-trivial, it may not always be obvious what the List contains.

The other point to notice about the preceding code—and it's actually the main point—is that the code will compile without problems. You'll only discover the error at runtime. There was no way for the compiler to warn us that we're about to do something that is not type-safe. This is the main problem that generics is trying to solve. Type-safety.

Going back to Listing 7-1, we know that the variable *v* is a List. It would have been more useful if we knew what kinds of things were stored on that list—this is where generics is helpful. It allows us to say things like "this is a list of Strings" or "this is a list of Ints"—and the compiler knows that beforehand; and because the compiler knows it, it can prevent us from doing inappropriate things like casting a String to an Int or doing substraction operation with Strings, etc. Listing 7-2 shows how to use generics in our code.

Listing 7-2. List, with Generics. Java

```
List<String> v = new ArrayList<String>();
v.add("test");
Integer i = v.get(0); // (type error)  compilation-time error
```

Now that the compiler has foreknowledge what kind of things are in the List, it can prevent us from doing unsupported operations.

The codes in Listings 7-1 and 7-2 are both valid in Java, which means you have the option not to use generics in Collections (*raw types*). Java had to do it because it needed to maintain backward compatibility with codes that were written prior to JDK 5. Kotlin on the other hand doesn't need to maintain any compatibilities with legacy codes. So, in Kotlin, you cannot use *raw types*. All Kotlin Collections require type parameters. You always have to use generics.

Terminologies

Generic programming is a language feature of Kotlin. With it, we can define classes, functions, and interfaces that accept type parameters. The parameterized type lets re-use the algorithm to work with different types, it truly is, a form of *parametric polymorphism*. Figure 7-1 shows where the type parameters and type arguments are found in a generic class.

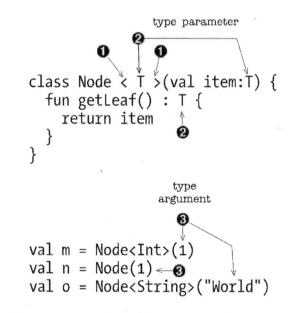

Figure 7-1. *Type arguments and type parameters*

❶ **Angle brackets** – When a class has angle brackets at the end of its name, it's called a generic class (there are also generic functions and interfaces).

❷ **Type parameter** – It defines the type of data that this class can work with. You can think of it as being part of the class implementation. Right now, we're using the letter **T** to symbolize the type parameter, but this is arbitrary. You can call it anything you want, it can be any letter or a combination of letters; I use **T** because it's the convention many developers follow. You can use **T** throughout the code inside the class as if it's a real type. It's a *placeholder* for a type. In this example, we used **T** as type for the **item** property and as return type for the **getLeaf** function.

❸ **Type argument** – In order to use the generic class, you have to provide the **type argument**. Now that we're creating an instance of the Node class, **T** will be substituted by *type argument* (*Int* and *String*, in this illustration).

You've seen generics code in the previous chapters, specifically in Chapter 6, "Collections". All of Kotlin's collections classes use generics. There are no raw types in Kotlin, so it's not possible to create just a *List*, you have to be specific what kind of *List* it is, for example, a "list of Strings" **List<String>** or "a list of Ints" **List<Int>**.

Using Generics in Functions

To create a generic function, declare the type parameter before the function name. Then, you can use the type parameter anywhere in the function.

Listing 7-3. fooBar, generic function

```
fun <T> fooBar(arg:T) : String { ❶
  return "Heya $arg"  // ❷
}
```

```
println(fooBar("Joe"))   // prints "Heya Joe"
println(fooBar(10))      // prints "Heya 10"
```

---

❶   The type parameter **T** is used as the type of the function parameter **arg**.

❷   We're just returning the **arg** concatenated in String.

In the preceding code, we just used the type param in one place and the function is returning a String, no matter what type the param is. Let's see another example, see Listing 7-4.

Listing 7-4. A more complex fooBar function

```
fun <T> fooBar(arg:T) : T {  ❶
  var retval:T = 0 as T
  when (arg) {
    is String -> {            ❷
      retval = "Hello world" as T  ❸
    }
    is Number -> {
      retval = 100 as T
    }
  }
  return retval
}
```

---

❶   In this example, we used the *type parameter* as a type for **arg** (parameter to **fooBar** function) and as a return type of the function itself.

❷   We're testing if **arg** is of String type. If it is, we're also effectively casting it to a String; smart cast, remember?

❸   We're returning "Hello world", and were casting it (forcibly) as **T**. We cannot return a "String" type right here, because fooBar expects to return type **T** to its caller, not String.

You can also use generics for extension functions. If you're making a function that works with Lists, you probably want it to work with any kind of List, not just Strings or Ints. Listing 7-5 shows how to use generics in an extension function.

Listing 7-5. Generics in extension function

```
fun <T> List<T>.getIt(index:Int): T { ❶
  return this[index] ❷
}

fun main(args: Array<String>) {
  val lfruits = listOf("Apples", "Bananas", "Oranges") ❸
  val lnumbers = listOf(1,3,5)      ❹
  val lnumlist = (1..100).toList().filter { it % 5 == 0 } ❺

  println(lnumlist.getIt(5))
  println(lfruits.getIt(1))
}
```

❶ You can use the type parameter in the receiver (List<T>) and the return type of the extension function.

❷ Let's just return an item given an index. In a production code, you might want to actually check if the index exists, before you return it. In case you forgot what **this** refers to, it refers to the List itself (it's the receiver object).

❸ Our extension function works with a list of Strings.

❹ It also works with a list of Ints.

❺ This statement still returns a List, so our extension function should still work.

Using Generics in Classes

Like in Java, you can create Kotlin generic classes by putting a pair of angle brackets after the name of the class and placing the type parameter between the angle brackets. After that, you can use the type parameter anywhere in the class. Listing 7-6 shows, annotates, and explains how to write a generic class.

Listing 7-6. Writing a generic class

```kotlin
class Node<T>(val item:T) {     ❶
  fun getLeaf() : T {           ❷
    return item
  }
}

fun main(args: Array<String>) {
  val m = Node<Int>(1)              ❸
  val n = Node(1)                   ❹
  val o = Node<String>("World")     ❺
}
```

❶ Type parameter is declared right after the name of the class, **Node<T>**. We're using the **T** as the type for parameter **item**.

❷ We're also using **T** as the return value of the function **getLeaf**.

❸ We're passing an Int to the constructor of Node. We can be verbose and specify Int as the as the type parameter, **Node<Int>**.

❹ The Node class can infer what the type parameter is, so we can skip the angle brackets. It's okay to write it this way too.

❺ And because it's a generic class, it works with Strings too.

You can constrain or restrict the types that can be used as type arguments for a class or function. Our Node class, at the moment, should work with any type—because the default parent (or *upper bound*) for the type parameter, if you don't specify a constraint, is **Any?** (Nullable type, so the question mark is included).

When you specify an upper bound constraint for a type parameter, that will limit the types you can use to instantiate the class. For example, if we wanted our Node class to accept only Ints, Doubles, or Floats, we can use Number as the upper bound constraint. See Listing 7-7 for the code sample.

Listing 7-7. Node class, with constraint

```
class Node<T:Number>(val item:T) { ❶
  fun getLeaf() : T {
    return item
  }
}

fun main(args: Array<String>) {
  val m = Node<Int>(1)            ❷
  val n = Node(1.0F)              ❸
  val o = Node<String>("World")   ❹
  val p = Node(1.0)              ❺
}
```

---

❶ Now we're putting a constraint on the type parameter **<T:Number>**. The only types we can use to instantiate this class have to be subtypes of **Number**

❷ Int is subtype of Number, so it's okay.

❸ Float is also okay.

❹ This wouldn't work anymore, IntelliJ will tell you that "Type argument is not within bounds".

❺ This should still work for Double, since it is a child class of number.

If you don't have any restriction other than nullability of the type argument, you can simply use **Any** as the upper bound for the type parameter, see Listing 7-8.

Listing 7-8. Prevent null type arguments

```
class Node<T:Any>(val item:T) {
  fun getLeaf() : T {
    return item
  }
}
```

Variance

We'll need to review some of our OOP basics to prepare us for a discussion on variance. Hopefully, we can jog your memory and remember some of the fundamental principles of object-oriented programming.

OOP is boon to developers, because of it, we can write codes like Listing 7-9.

Listing 7-9. Assign an Int variable to Number type

```
val a:Int =  1
val b:Number = a

println("b:$b is of type ${b.javaClass.name}")
```

We can also write functions like in Listing 7-10.

Listing 7-10. Function that accepts a Number type

```
foo(1)
foo(100F)
foo(120)

fun foo(arg:Number) {
  println(arg)
}
```

The codes in Listings 7-9 and 7-10 are possible because of the *Liskov Substitution Principle* (LSP). It's one of the more important parts of OOP—where a parent type is expected, you can use a subtype in its place. The reason we use a more generalized type (like **Number**, in Listing 7-10) is so that in the future, if we need to, we can write an implementation of a subtype and insert into an existing and working code. This is the essence of the **Open Closed Principle** (which states that a class must be open to extension but closed to modification).

Note   The **Liskov Substitution Principle** and **Open Closed Principle** are part of the SOLID design principles. It's one of the more popular sets of design principles in OOP. SOLID stands for (S) Single Responsibility (O) Open Closed (L) Liskov Substitution (I) Interface Segregation and (D) Dependency Inversion.

Let's take another example, see Listing 7-11.

Listing 7-11. Employee, Programmer, and Tester

```
open class Employee(val name:String) {
  override fun toString(): String {
    return name
  }
}

class Programmer(name:String) : Employee(name) {}
class Tester(name:String) : Employee(name) {}

fun main(args: Array<String>) {
  val employee_1 :Employee = Programmer("Ted")   ❶
  val employee_2 :Employee = Tester("Steph")     ❷

  println(employee_1)
  println(employee_2)
}
```

❶ employee_1 is of type **Employee**, we're assigning a **Programmer** object to it. Which is okay. Programmer is a *subtype* of Employee.

❷ Same thing here, the type **Tester** is a subtype of **Employee**, so the assignment should be okay.

No surprises here, the Liskov principle is still at work. Even if you put Programmer and Employee on a List, the type relationship is preserved.

Listing 7-12. Employee and Programmer in Lists

```
val list_1: List<Programmer> = listOf(Programmer("James"))
val list_2: List<Employee> = list_1
```

So far so good, what about this next code, do you think it will work? (Listing 7-13).

Listing 7-13. Group of Employees and Programmers

```
class Group<T>
val a:Group<Employee> = Group<Programmer>()
```

This is one of the tricky parts of generics. Listing 7-13, as it currently stands, won't work. Even if we know that **Programmer** is a subtype of **Employee**, and that what we're doing is type safe, the compiler won't let us through because the second statement in the preceding code has a problem.

When you're working with generics, always remember that by default **Group<Employee>**, **Group<Programmer>**, and **Group<Tester>** don't have any type relationship—even if we know that Tester and Programmer are subtypes of Employee. By default, the type parameter in the class **Group<T>** is *invariant*. For the second statement (in Listing 7-13) to work, **Group<T>** has to be *covariant*. We'll solve in Listing 7-14.

Listing 7-14. Classes Employee, Programmer, Tester, and Group

```
class Group<out T>      ❶

open class Employee(val name:String) {
  override fun toString(): String {
    return name
  }
}
class Programmer(name:String) : Employee(name) {}
class Tester(name:String) : Employee(name) {}

fun main(args: Array<String>) {
  val a:Group<Employee> = Group<Programmer>() ❷
}
```

❶ When you put the **out** keyword before the type parameter, that makes the type parameter *covariant.*

❷ This code works because, **Group<Programmer>** is *now* a subtype of **Group<Employee>**, thanks to the **out** keyword.

From these examples, we can now generalize that if type Programmer is a subtype of Employee and **Group<T>** is covariant, then **Group<Programmer>** is a subtype of **Group<Employee>.** Also, we can generalize that generic class, like Group, is invariant on type parameter, if for the given types **Employee** and **Programmer**, **Group<Programmer>** isn't a subtype of **Group<Employee>.**

Now we've dealt with *invariant* and *covariant.* The last terminology we need to deal with is *contravariant.* If the type parameter of **Group<T>** is contravariant, for the same given types Employee and Programmer, then we can say that **Group<Employee>** is a subtype of **Group<Programmer>**—it's quite the reverse of *covariant.*

Listing 7-15. Use the in keyword for contravariance

```
class Group<in T> ❶

open class Employee(val name:String) {
  override fun toString(): String {
    return name
  }
}
class Programmer(name:String) : Employee(name) {}
class Tester(name:String) : Employee(name) {}

fun main(args: Array<String>) {
  val a:Group<Programmer> = Group<Employee>()  ❷
}
```

❶   The **in** keyword makes the type parameter <T> contravariant, which means;

❷   type **Group<Employee>** is now a subtype of **Group<Programmer>**

Reified Generics

Reify means to make something real, and the reason we're using reify and generics on the same statement is because of Java's *type erasure*.

Type erasure means exactly what it implies. Java—and Kotlin as well—erases generic type information at runtime. There are good reasons for this, but unfortunately, we're not going to discuss those reasons why the language design is like that—but we will discuss its effects. Because of type erasure, you can't perform any reflection activity and you can't do any runtime check on a type, if it's generic. See Listing 7-16 for an example.

Listing 7-16. Check for type at runtime

```
fun checkInfo(items:List<Any>) {
    if(items is List<String>) {        ❶
       println("item is a list of Strings")
    }
  }
}
```

❶ This won't compile. The error is "*Cannot check for instance of erased type*".

The **is** keyword doesn't work on generic types at runtime, the smart cast breaks because of type erasure. If you have some confidence about what the runtime type of the List will be, you can make a speculative decision and cast it using the **as** keyword, like this

```
val i = item as List<String>
```

The compiler will let you through, but this is a dangerous thing to do. Let's consider one more example where we can build a stronger case as to why we need to retain type information at runtime.

Let's say I have a List of objects, Programmer and Tester objects. I want to create a function where I can pass a type parameter and filter the list using that type parameter. I want the function to return the filtered list. Listing 7-17 shows us a code sample on how this might be done—the code sample won't work of course, because of the type erasure issue, but just read through it first, we will fix it later.

Listing 7-17. Filtering a list using a type parameter

```kotlin
fun main(args: Array<String>) {
  val mlist = listOf(Programmer("Ted"), Tester("Steph"))     ❶
  val mprogs = mlist.typeOf<Programmer>()                     ❷

  mprogs.forEach {                                           ❸
    println("${it.toString()} : ${it.javaClass.simpleName}")
  }
}

fun <T> List<*>.typeOf() : List<T> {                         ❹

  val retlist = mutableListOf<T>()                           ❺
  this.forEach {
    if (it is T) {                                           ❻
      retlist.add(it)                                        ❼
    }
  }
  return retlist                                             ❽
}
```

```
open class Employee(val name:String) {
  override fun toString(): String {
    return name
  }
}
class Programmer(name:String) : Employee(name) {}
class Tester(name:String) : Employee(name) {}
```

---

❶   Let's create a list of Programmer and Tester objects.

❷   Let's call an extension function (of the List type) called **typeOf**. We're passing **Programmer** as a type argument, which means, we want this function to return only a list of Programmers objects.

❸   We're just iterating through each item of the list. We print the *name* property and the Java simpleName.

❹   Now we come to the definition of the extension function. We're defining a type parameter <T>, we're using **T** as the return type of this function. Also, we want this function to work with any kind of List, hence the syntax.

❺   Let's define a mutable list, we'll use this to hold the filtered list.

❻   This is the code that won't compile because we don't know what kind of List is this anymore at runtime. Kotlin, like Java, erases the type information. But let's assume for a moment that Kotlin does retain generic type information; if that's the case, then this code is okay.

❼   If the condition is okay, let's add the current item to the return value.

❽   Finally, let's return the filtered list.

Listing 7-17 would have worked perfectly if only **List.typeOf** can remember, at runtime, what kind of list it is. To solve this problem, we'll use the *inline* and *reified* keyword. Listing 7-18 shows us how to do this.

Listing 7-18. How to use reified and inline in a function

```kotlin
inline fun <reified T> List<*>.typeOf() : List<T> { ❶
  val retlist = mutableListOf<T>()
  this.forEach {
    if (it is T) {
      retlist.add(it)
    }
  }
  return retlist
}
```

---

❶ Make the function **inline** and use the **reified** keyword before the type
   parameter. After doing this, the function can retain type information at runtime.

When you inline a function, the compiler will replace every call to
that function with the actual code implementing the function—it's like
copying and pasting the code implementation of the function all over the
place. This, of course, will increase the size of your runtime program, so
use it sparingly. Listing 7-19 shows the full and revised code of the reified
example.

Listing 7-19. Filtering a list using a type parameter

```kotlin
fun main(args: Array<String>) {
  val mlist = listOf(Programmer("Ted"), Tester("Steph"))
  val mprogs = mlist.typeOf<Programmer>()

  mprogs.forEach {
    println("${it.toString()} : ${it.javaClass.simpleName}")
  }
}
```

```kotlin
inline fun <reified T> List<*>.typeOf() : List<T> {

  val retlist = mutableListOf<T>()
  this.forEach {
    if (it is T) {
      retlist.add(it)
    }
  }
  return retlist
}

open class Employee(val name:String) {
  override fun toString(): String {
    return name
  }
}
class Programmer(name:String) : Employee(name) {}
class Tester(name:String) : Employee(name) {}
```

Key Takeaways

- Generic programming lets us reuse algorithms.

- All Collections in Kotlin use generics.

- Kotlin doesn't have raw types, like Java.

- There are three variances you need to know about: 1) invariance, 2) covariance, and 3) contravariance.

- Kotlin, like Java, erases generic type information at runtime; but if you want to retain type information, inline your functions and use the reified keyword.

CHAPTER 8

Debugging

All but the most trivial programs are without errors (the first time you write them). Dealing with errors will be a big part of your life as a developer.

What we'll cover:

- Error types

- Using the Debugger

- Other uses for the Debugger

Errors

While you're coding, you'll likely experience 1) syntax errors, 2) runtime errors, and 3) logic errors.

Syntax errors happen because you put something in the code that's not allowed in the set of rules of the compiler. The compiler doesn't understand it. The error can be as simple as forgetting to close a parenthesis or a missing pair of curly braces. It can also be complex, like passing the wrong type of argument to a function or a parameterized class when using generics.

A good IDE should spot and, more importantly, help you correct syntax errors. Figure 8-1 shows IntelliJ pointing out an error. When you see red squiggly lines adorning your codes, it means IntelliJ spotted syntax errors.

© Ted Hagos 2023
T. Hagos, *Beginning Kotlin*, https://doi.org/10.1007/978-1-4842-8698-2_8

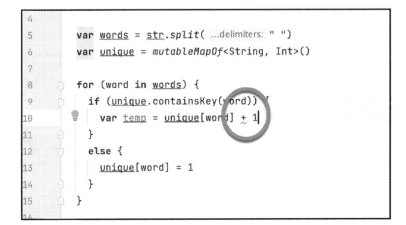

Figure 8-1. *Editor showing an error indicator*

The syntax error shown in Figure 8-1 shows an attempt to invoke the
.plus(1) extension function on a nullable receiver—which is not allowed
in Kotlin; that's why the editor is calling our attention.

With a good IDE, you can dispense with syntax errors without much
difficulty. You can usually fix syntax errors in IntelliJ by using Alt + Enter.
The problem-solving shortcut is shown in action in Figure 8-2.

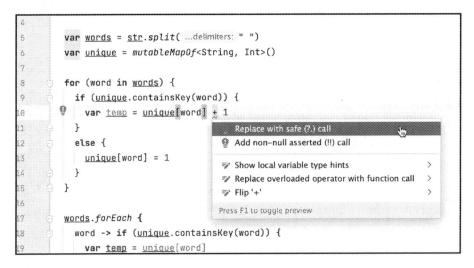

Figure 8-2. *Context action showed after using Alt + Enter*

If you can only memorize two keyboard shortcuts in IntelliJ, let the first one be **Alt + Enter** (triggers context actions) and the second one be **Shift + Shift** (which lets you search everywhere).

Whenever you see squiggly lines or yellow or red light bulbs in the IDEA editor, press `Alt + Enter` because the editor has some help to offer.

Runtime and Logic Errors

Runtime and logic errors happen while your program is running. The compiler cannot help you with these errors because static analysis (of the code) is not very helpful during runtime. This is where the Debugger becomes useful.

Working the Debugger

Let's try a simple debugging case. Consider the sample code in Listing 8-1. It's a short program that counts the frequency of each word in a given string.

Listing 8-1. WordFrequency.kt

```
fun main(args:Array<String>) {
  var str = "the quick brown fox the quick brown fox
  jumped over"

  var words = str.split(" ")                    //#1
  var unique = mutableMapOf<String, Int>()      //#2

  words.forEach {                               //#3
    word -> if (unique.containsKey(word)) {     //#4
      var temp = unique[word]
      temp =+ 1
      unique[word] = temp                       //#5
    }
```

```
    else {
      unique.put(word, 1)                              //#6
    }
  }
}

  println(unique)                                      //#7
}
```

> **#1** Split the string using the white space as a delimiter and store it in a List.
>
> **#2** We'd like a mutable Map to store the unique words and count their frequency.
>
> **#3** Walk through each element of the *words* array.
>
> **#4** Let's check if the current word already exists in the *unique* Map.
>
> **#5** If the current word exists in the *unique* Map, let's get its current value and increment it by one and put it back in the Map.
>
> **#6** If the current word isn't on the unique Map yet, let's create an entry for it, then set its value to 1.
>
> **#7** Let's print the contents of the unique Map.

The sample program compiles and runs without issues, but as it stands, it has a bug. The output should be like this

```
{the=2, quick=2, brown=2, fox=2, jumped=1, over=1}
```

Instead, it prints the following output:

```
{the=1, quick=1, brown=1, fox=1, jumped=1, over=1}
```

Debugging is detective work. You cannot wantonly set breakpoints just anywhere. You have to mentally work out where is a good starting point to investigate.

The print statements aren't likely the suspects here. The code populates the Map; that much is obvious; otherwise, we won't see any printed values of it. The likely culprit is the block of code where we increment the value of existing entries in the *unique* Map. See Figure 8-3.

```kotlin
2  ▶  fun main(args:Array<String>) {
3          var str = "the quick brown fox the quick brown fox jumped over"
4
5          var words = str.split( ...delimiters: " ")
6          var unique = mutableMapOf<String, Int>()
7
8          words.forEach {
9              word -> if (unique.containsKey(word)) {
10                 var temp = unique[word]
11                 temp =+ 1
12                 unique[word] = temp
13             }
14             else {
15                 unique.put(word, 1)
16             }
17         }
18
19         println(unique)
20     }
```

Figure 8-3. *Suspected block of code*

We'll start the investigation between lines 9–12 (as shown in Figure 8-2).

Set Breakpoints

To examine how our code works at runtime, we will suspend the execution before the suspected piece of code. You do this by setting breakpoints.

When you set a breakpoint, code execution suspends at that location, so you can poke around and examine various aspects of the program.

Click the gutter line where you want to set the breakpoint. In our case, we'll set it at the beginning of the *if* block, as shown in Figure 8-4. The breakpoint appears as a big red dot in the editor gutter—it may not appear as red in Figure 8-3, but it is red.

```
 2  ▶   fun main(args:Array<String>) {
 3          var str = "the quick brown fox the quick brown fox jumped over"
 4
 5          var words = str.split( ...delimiters: " ")
 6          var unique = mutableMapOf<String, Int>()
 7
 8          words.forEach {
 9  ●           word -> if (unique.containsKey(word)) {
10                  var temp = unique[word]
11                  temp =+ 1
12                  unique[word] = temp
13              }
14              else {
15                  unique.put(word, 1)
16              }
17          }
18
19          println(unique)
20      }
```

Figure 8-4. *Breakpoint set at line 9*

Run the Program in Debug Mode

Once we've set the breakpoint, it's time to run the program—in Debug mode, of course. To be sure, IntelliJ has more than one way of running the code in Debug mode. You can use the toolbar button. See Figure 8-5.

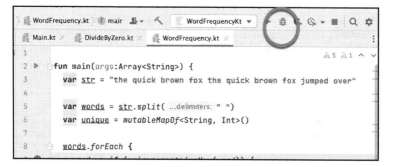

Figure 8-5. *Debug button on the toolbar*

Or you can press **CTRL + D** (if you're on macOS) or **Shift + F9** (if you're on a PC). Alternatively, you can use the Run button on the gutter. Figure 8-6 shows a (green) arrow on the gutter, right next to fun main().

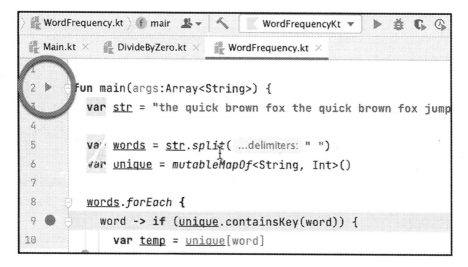

Figure 8-6. *Run button on the gutter*

When you click the Run button in the gutter, you can choose whether to Run, Debug, Run with Coverage, Profile or Modify the Run configuration of the current program (as shown in Figure 8-7). Choose the **Debug** option to proceed.

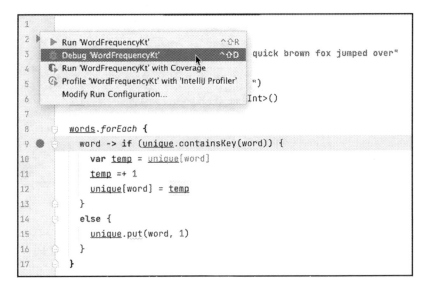

Figure 8-7.   *Run the program in Debug mode*

Analyze the Program State

During the debugging session, the program runs normally until it hits the breakpoint. When this happens, IntelliJ highlights the line where the program paused. See Figure 8-8.

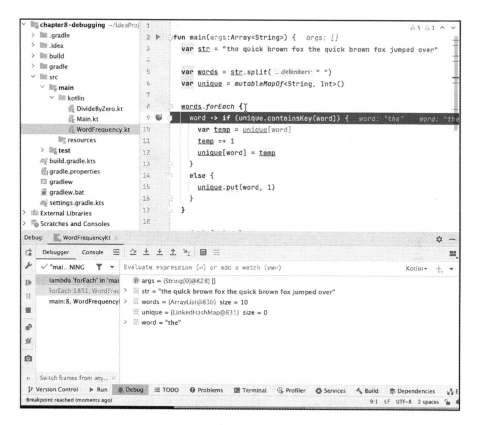

Figure 8-8. *Debugger session paused*

The highlighted line is yet to execute. IntelliJ is waiting for instructions from you. While the code is in a suspended state, you can examine variables that hold the state of the program, as shown in Figure 8-9.

Figure 8-9. Variables show their current values in the Debug window

At this point, we can see the *args, str, words (List), unique (Map),* and *word (the iterator)* variables. Our Map structure shows zero size because we haven't populated it at this point yet. Remember, we placed the breakpoint at the beginning of the if block, which means we're evaluating the very first word in our *List* structure.

Now, we single step into the code. Figure 8-10 shows the Debugger window.

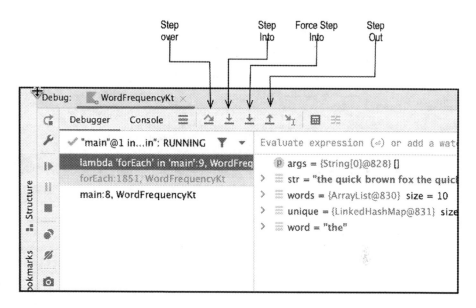

Figure 8-10. *The Debugger window*

There are many buttons on the Debugger tool window. There are buttons to stop/start and restart the debug sessions—you can quickly discover them yourself. There are also buttons for single-stepping into the current code.

The *Step Into* and *Step Over* actions are very similar. They both execute the next line of command. But in the case of *Step Over*, if the next line is a function call, the Debugger executes the function and returns the result without debugging each line. In contrast, the *Step Into* action debugs each line, including that of the individual statements inside the function.

In our case, all the lines of code we want to debug are within function main; we don't have any other function; we can use either the *Step Into* or the *Step Over* action.

Using the Step Into action brings us to the next line (Figure 8-11).

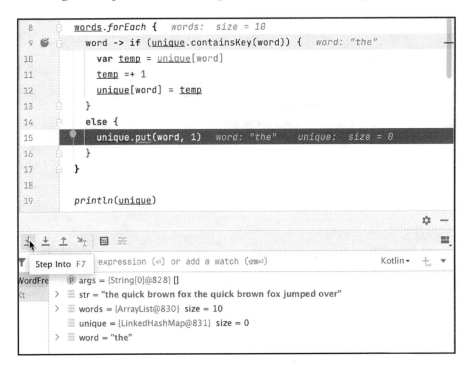

Figure 8-11. *Steps into the next line*

The program was still paused, but we stepped into the next line. The condition on the if() block fails because the unique Map doesn't contain the word "the" (first word on the List). So, the program execution takes us into the *else* clause. Let's step into the next line. Figure 8-12 shows where the program is paused next.

```
 8        words.forEach {   words:  size = 10
 9          word -> if (unique.containsKey(word)) {  word: "the"
10            var temp = unique[word]
11            temp =+ 1
12            unique[word] = temp
13          }
14          else {
15            unique.put(word, 1)   word: "the"   unique: size = 1
16          }
17

18
19        println(unique)
```

Evaluate expression (↵) or add a watch (⌥⌘↵)   Kotlin▾

WordFre   ℗ args = {String[0]@828} []
t   > ▤ str = "the quick brown fox the quick brown fox jumped over"
           > ▤ words = {ArrayList@830} size = 10
           > ▤ unique = {LinkedHashMap@831} size = 1
           > ▤ word = "the"

Figure 8-12. *Steps into the next line*

Notice that our unique (Map) variable now contains one element. This is right after we added the first word to the List.

We're now at the end of the forEach loop. Stepping again takes us to the beginning of the loop. Stepping again takes us to the *if* block.

If we keep on stepping, eventually, our program reaches the point where the test for unique.containsKey(word) will return true—when it hits the word "the" for the second time (shown in Figure 8-13).

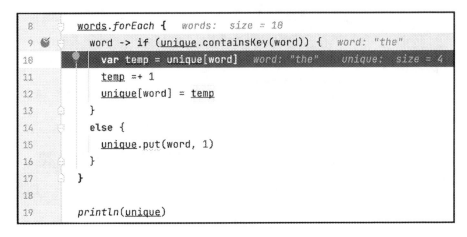

```
8         words.forEach {   words:  size = 10
9         word -> if (unique.containsKey(word) {  word: "the"
10            var temp = unique[word]   word: "the"    unique:  size = 4
11            temp =+ 1
12            unique[word] = temp
13        }
14        else {
15            unique.put(word, 1)
16        }
17    }
18
19    println(unique)
```

Figure 8-13. *Steps into the next line*

Now the test on the if block evaluates to true. We then extract the current count of the current word. Let's step again. Figure 8-14 shows the debugger snapshot.

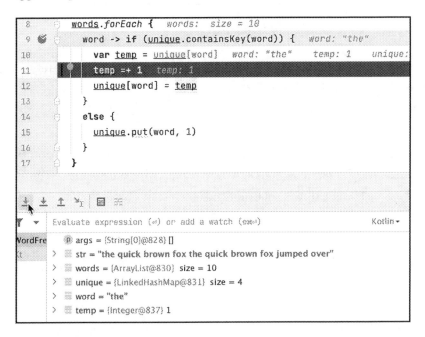

Figure 8-14. *Steps into the next line*

We have a new variable (temp) in scope; its current value is one. Let's step again. Figure 8-15 shows the next snapshot.

```
8        words.forEach {   words:  size = 10
9           word -> if (unique.containsKey(word)) {   word: "the"
10             var temp = unique[word]   temp: 1
11             temp =+ 1
12             unique[word] = temp   word: "the"   temp: 1   unique:   si
13          }
14          else {              I
15             unique.put(word, 1)
16          }
17       }
18
19       println(unique)
```

```
Evaluate expression (↵) or add a watch (⌥⌘↵)                    Kotlin ▾

ⓟ args = {String[0]@828} []
>   str = "the quick brown fox the quick brown fox jumped over"
>   words = {ArrayList@830} size = 10
>   unique = {LinkedHashMap@831} size = 4
>   word = "the"
>   temp = {Integer@837} 1
```

Figure 8-15. *Steps into the next line*

At this point, we're ready to put the updated count back into the *unique* (Map), but the value of *temp* doesn't look right. It's supposed to be two—not one—because we've already incremented it. This is where we take a closer look at the code. It's when you'll notice this line

```
temp =+ 1
```

This is the culprit. It's supposed to read like this

```
temp += 1
```

Kotlin didn't flag it as a syntax error because technically, `temp =+1` is a legit code; we're saying that we're setting the value of the temp variable to positive one (+1). This clearly was not our intention; we wanted instead to increment the *temp* variable by one.

Let's stop the Debug session and then fix the code. You can stop the Debugger by using the stop button on Debug tool window (shown in Figure 8-16).

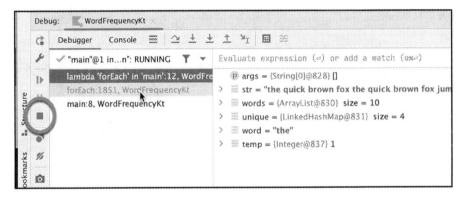

Figure 8-16. *Stop the Debugger*

Replacing the faulty increment operator in our code presented some new problems. As soon as you replace the =+ code with the proper += increment operator, IntelliJ flags a syntax error (shown in Figure 8-17).

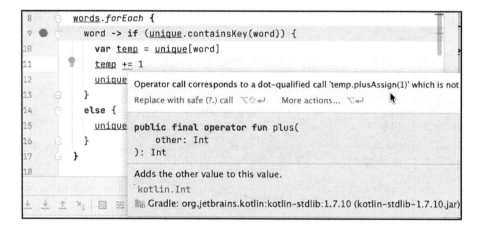

```
8        words.forEach {
9            word -> if (unique.containsKey(word)) {
10               var temp = unique[word]
11               temp += 1
12               unique  Operator call corresponds to a dot-qualified call 'temp.plusAssign(1)' which is not
13           }            Replace with safe (?.) call  ⌥⇧↵    More actions...  ⌥↵        ↖
14           else {
15               unique  public final operator fun plus(
16           }                   other: Int
17       }            ): Int

18                        Adds the other value to this value.
                         kotlin.Int
↓ ↓ ↥ ×ᵣ  □ ⇥    Gradle: org.jetbrains.kotlin:kotlin-stdlib:1.7.10 (kotlin-stdlib-1.7.10.jar)
```

Figure 8-17. *Syntax issue with the increment operator*

While Kotlin prevents us from ever encountering null pointer errors, there are still some occasions where this is unavoidable. Kotlin collections are direct instances of Java collections, and the Map get() method may return a null value. We cannot declare the *temp* variable as a non-nullable Int because we're assigning it a value that may potentially return null. That's why we're being flagged.

To fix this, let's follow the suggestion of the context action; let's replace the statement with a safe call. Listing 8-2 shows the corrected code.

Listing 8-2. WordFrequency.kt, corrected

```kotlin
fun main(args:Array<String>) {
  var str = "the quick brown fox the quick brown fox
jumped over"

  var words = str.split(" ")
  var unique: MutableMap<String, Int> =
mutableMapOf<String, Int>()

  words.forEach {
    word -> if (unique.containsKey(word)) {
```

```
    var temp: Int? = unique[word]
    temp = temp?.plus(1)!!
    unique[word] = temp
  }
  else {
    unique.put(word, 1)
  }
}
println(unique)
}
```

Running the program now gives us the expected output:

```
{the=2, quick=2, brown=2, fox=2, jumped=1, over=1}
```

Other Uses of the Debugger

Programmers typically use the debugger when looking for bugs; for a good reason, the tool is aptly named. But the debugger can function beyond mere bug-hunting. You can use the Debugger to:

- **Fix and find bugs** – We did this in the previous section.

- **Code analysis** – You can view which parts of the code get executed using the Debugger's single-step tools. You can even inspect the program state (variable values) at any time. Also, by using the single-step tool of the Debugger, you can familiarize yourself with the code. This can be particularly useful when you're inheriting old code from somebody else or using code from another team (or company).

- **Change the program state** – I don't mean to change the source code during the Debug sessions; what I mean is you can change the values of member variables (or any variable for that matter) while in Debug session. This lets you reproduce some complicated setups on the fly; for example, if your app is expected to behave one way depending on certain states (state machines), you can quickly achieve this during a Debug session—because you can change the values of the variables during the session. There won't be any need to edit the source code and go through restart cycles manually. It can save you time.

- **More logging on the fly, no need to restart or recompile.**

Changing the Program State

Consider the code in Listing 8-3. It's a simplistic code, but it's enough to demonstrate how we can change the program state during a Debug session.

Listing 8-3. DivideByZero.kt

```kotlin
fun main(args: Array<String>) {

  var dividend = Integer.parseInt(args[0])
  var divisor = Integer.parseInt(args[1])

  println("Quotient = ${divide(dividend, divisor)}");

}

fun divide(a:Int,b:Int): Int {
  return a/b
}
```

To start the Debug session, let's set the breakpoint after we've declared the dividend variable (shown in Figure 8-18).

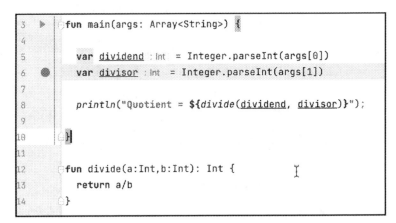

Figure 8-18. *Set the breakpoint*

The code expects some input from command line arguments. To pass the arguments, click the Run button (on the gutter), then choose Modify Run Configuration, as shown in Figure 8-19.

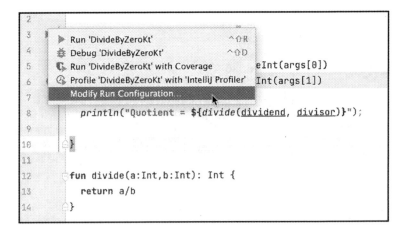

Figure 8-19. *Modify Run Configuration*

In the following screen, pass the program arguments, as shown in Figure 8-20.

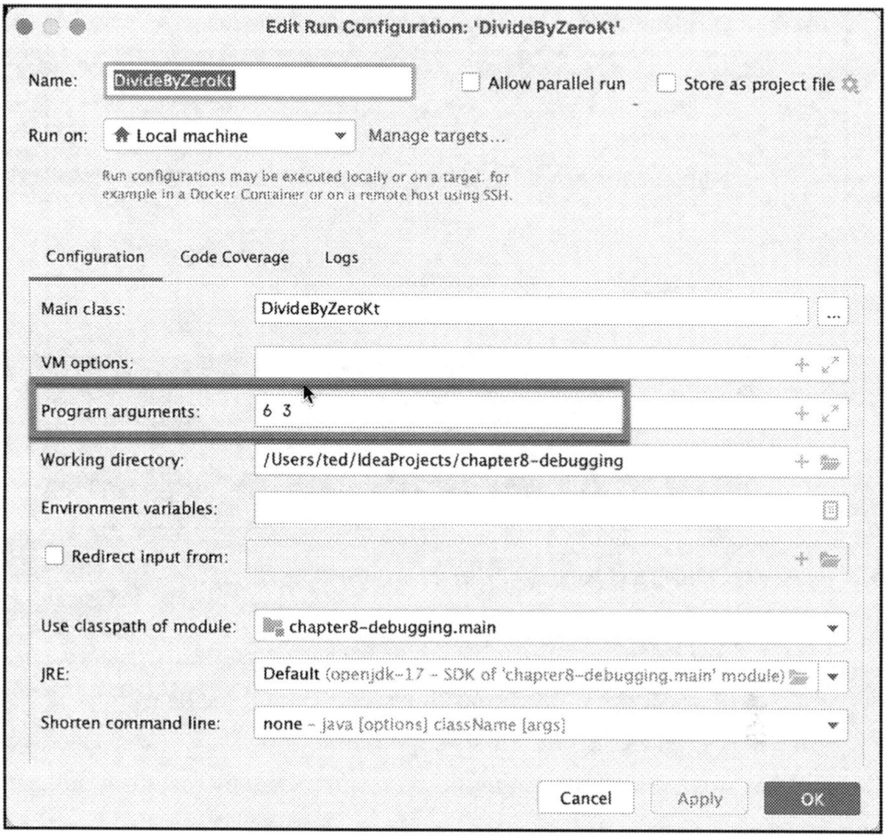

Figure 8-20. *Program arguments*

The program expects two arguments. We're passing the two arguments separating them by space.

Click **Ok** to proceed. Then, start the Debug session. As expected, the runtime pauses when it hits the breakpoint. This gives us a chance to inspect the app's state. See Figure 8-21.

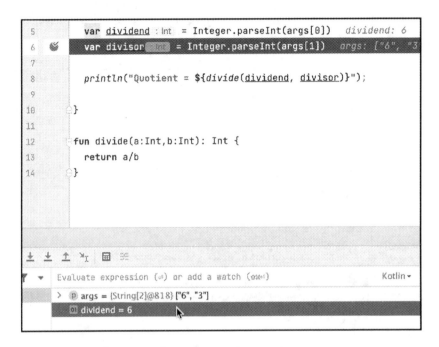

Figure 8-21. *Debug window shows the app's state*

The dividend shows a value equal to 6. No surprises there; that's what we passed in the program arguments. If we continue the execution, the program will print 2 as output. That's expected, but if you want to see alternative results, you can change the program's state by resetting the value of its variables.

You can change the value of the dividend variable by right-clicking on it (shown in Figure 8-22).

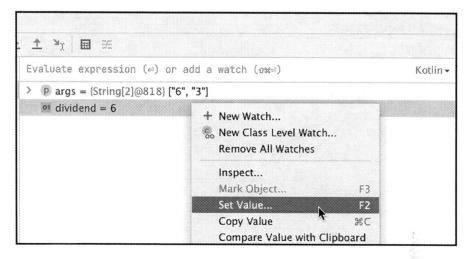

Figure 8-22. *Set the value of a variable in Debug session*

Type the new value. Then press **Enter**, as shown in Figure 8-23.

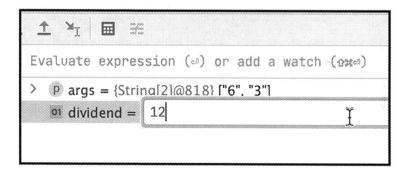

Figure 8-23. *Set the value of the variable*

Continue to step into the code until you reach the last statement, or simply resume the Debug session since we don't care about seeing the rest of the program in Debug mode. The resume button is located along the side toolbar of the Debug tool window (shown in Figure 8-24).

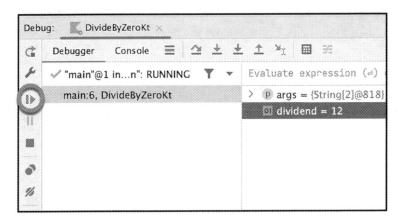

Figure 8-24. *Resume program*

Resuming the program continues the program execution. Since we don't have any more breakpoints, the program exits and prints the output (shown in Figure 8-25).

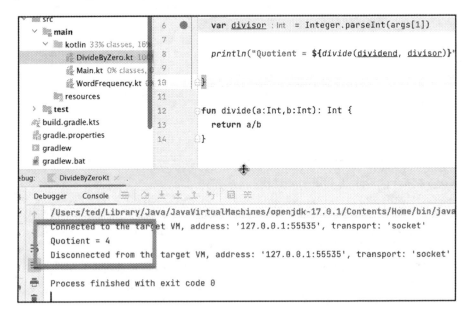

Figure 8-25. *App output*

The program should have printed "Quotient = 2", but since we change the dividend (variable) value to 12, the quotient is now 4.

Key Takeaways

- The Debugger has uses beyond mere bug-finding.

- You can gain valuable insights into your codes runtime behavior by using the single-step actions of the Debugger.

CHAPTER 9

Unit Testing

Unit testing is writing many small tests. Each test targets a function's behavior. Unit testing is the kind of testing that's done by a developer, not the QA.

What we'll cover:

- How to setup JUnit

- How to create a unit test

- How to write asserts

A unit test is simple. It tests a particular thing that a function might do or produce. An application typically has many unit tests because each test is a very narrowly defined set of behavior. So, you'll need lots of tests to cover the whole functionality. Developers usually use JUnit to write unit tests.

JUnit is a regression testing framework written by Kent Beck and Erich Gamma; you might remember them as the one who created extreme programming and the other one from Gang of Four (GoF, Design Patterns), respectively, among other things.

Java developers have long used JUnit for unit testing. IntelliJ comes with JUnit and is very well integrated into it. We don't have to do much by way of setup. We only need to write our tests. We will use Junit5.

© Ted Hagos 2023
T. Hagos, *Beginning Kotlin*, https://doi.org/10.1007/978-1-4842-8698-2_9

Create the First Test

Let's start with some sample code. Consider the following snippet:

```
import java.util.*

class Util {

  fun getAge (birthdate: Calendar): Int {
    return 0
  }
}
```

To create a test for this class, place the caret somewhere inside the body of class Util, then press cmd + Enter (for macOS) or Alt + Insert (for PC), then choose "Test", as shown in Figure 9-1.

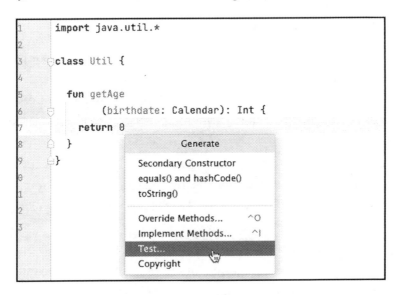

Figure 9-1. *Generate a test*

In the dialog that follows, you can choose the Testing library; let's use JUnit5. You'll notice the warning in the Create Test dialog (the yellow light bulb in Figure 9-2). It says, "JUnit library not found in the module". Click the **Fix** button to proceed.

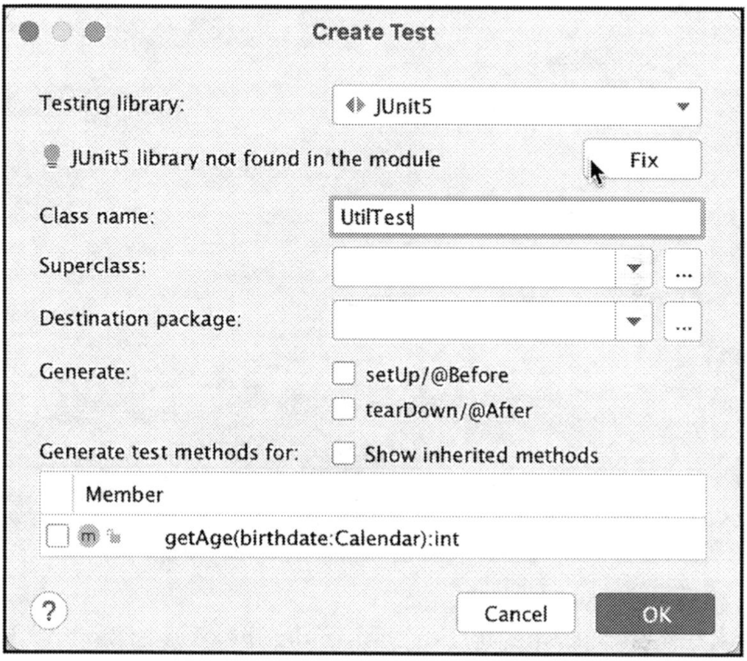

Figure 9-2. *Create Test*

After clicking the Fix button, IntelliJ will download the necessary files and sync the Gradle script; when that's done, the missing libraries warning disappears.

You can name the test (Class name) and choose the method you'd like to generate the test for (see Figure 9-3). I accepted the provided Class name (UtilTest) and checked the getAge() function in the member section.

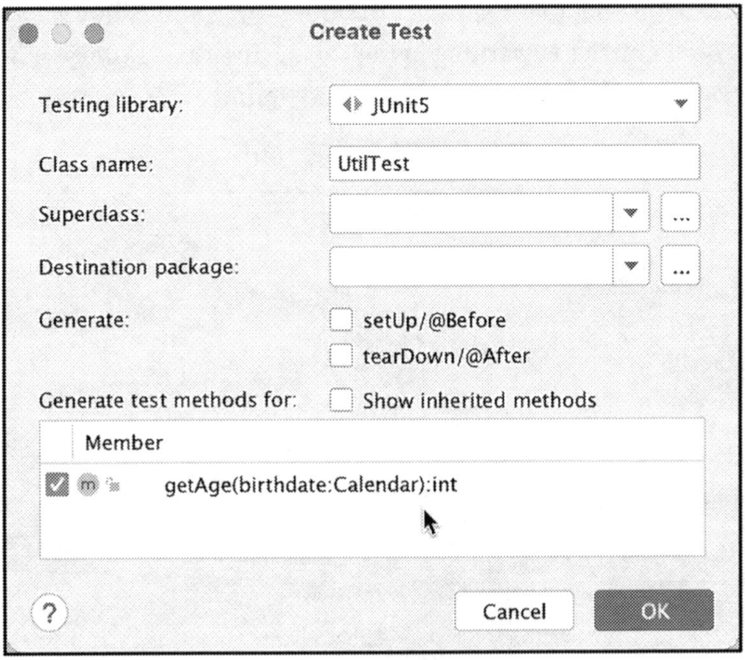

Figure 9-3.   *Create Test, Junit warning is fixed*

Click **OK** to proceed.

The IDE generates the UtilTest class under the src/test/kotlin folder (see Figure 9-4).

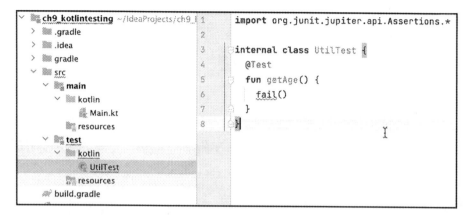

Figure 9-4. UtilTest.kt

The generated code has some problems. The IDE doesn't recognize the "@Test" annotation. You can fix this by importing the Test class. Use the Alt + Enter shortcut to pop the IDE's context suggestion (see Figure 9-5).

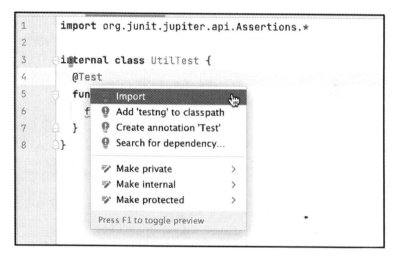

Figure 9-5. Import the Test class

Choose **Import**. Do the same for the fail() function (shown in Figure 9-6). We're importing the Test class from the JUnit5 packages.

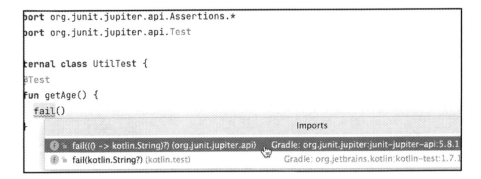

Figure 9-6. *Import the fail() function*

Here's the generated test function.

```
import org.junit.jupiter.api.Assertions.*
import org.junit.jupiter.api.Test
import kotlin.test.fail

internal class UtilTest {
  @Test                          //#1
  fun getAge() {
    fail()                       //#2
  }
}
```

#1 The getAge() function is annotated by @Test. This is how JUnit will know that getAge() is a unit test. You can prepend your function names with "Test", for example, getAgeTest(), but that's not necessary. The @Test annotation is enough.

#2 I put the fail() function here (it was not part of the generated test code). I placed it there. I thought, in the spirit of TDD, let's make the test fail first before we do anything else.

Let's run the test.

Like regular functions, you can also run tests using the arrow on the gutter (shown in Figure 9-7). To be sure, there's more than one way in

IntelliJ to Run a test. You can run it from the main menu bar (Run menu, then Run), from the toolbar, via a keyboard shortcut CTRL + R (macOS) or Shift + F10 (PC).

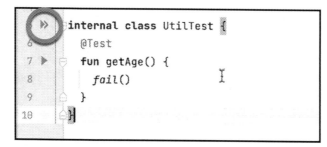

Figure 9-7. *Run the test*

Click the arrow on the gutter, then choose "Run UtilTest" (as shown in Figure 9-8).

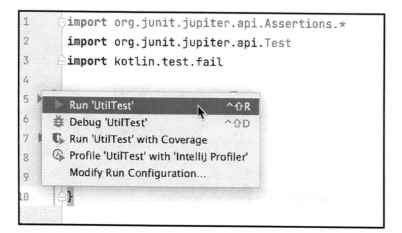

Figure 9-8. *Run UtilTest*

As you can see in the tool window (Figure 9-9), the test failed—as expected.

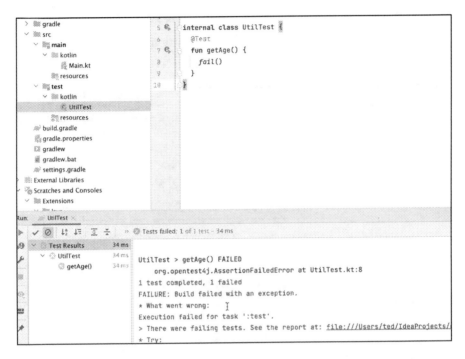

Figure 9-9. *Failed test*

Notice the icon on the gutter next to class UtilTest and the function getAge(); there are some extra icons. The green arrows are now joined by a red circle with an exclamation point—that signifies a failing test.

Write the Test Body

Let's write a proper test body now. Edit the test to match the code below:

```
internal class UtilTest {
  @Test
  fun checkWhenBornToday() {.                              //#1
    assertEquals(0, Util().getAge(Calendar.getInstance()))  //#2
  }
}
```

#1 Replace the generated function with checkWhenBornToday(). This is an apt name for a test if we want to know the age of someone born today.

#2 We expect getAge() to return zero if we pass a Calendar object that's initialized to the current date and time. The assertEquals() is one of the functions in JUnit; it returns true if two objects or primitives have the same value. We used the assert to find out if the first parameter (zero), which is the value we expect, will be equal to what getAge() will return. Let's see what the getAge() function will give us if we pass an instance of a Calendar object—the Calendar.getInstance() returns a Calendar object whose calendar fields were initialized to the current date and time.

The assertEquals is one of the assert functions you can use for unit tests; there are more asserts like assertFails, assertFailsWith, assertNotEquals, assertNotNull, etc. You can learn more assert functions from the Kotlin website https://kotlinlang.org/api/latest/kotlin.test/kotlin.test/. Here are some of them (Table 9-1).

Table 9-1. *Common assert functions provided by Kotlin*

Method	Description
assertEquals()	Returns true if two objects or primitives have the same value
assertNotEquals()	The reverse of assertEquals()
assertSame()	Returns true if two references point to the same object
assertNotSame()	Reverse of assertSame()
assertTrue()	Test a Boolean expression
assertFalse()	Reverse of assertTrue()
assertNull()	Test for a null object
assertNotNull()	Reverse of assertNull()

Run the Test

Let's run the test again. Click the arrow on the gutter (Figure 9-10).

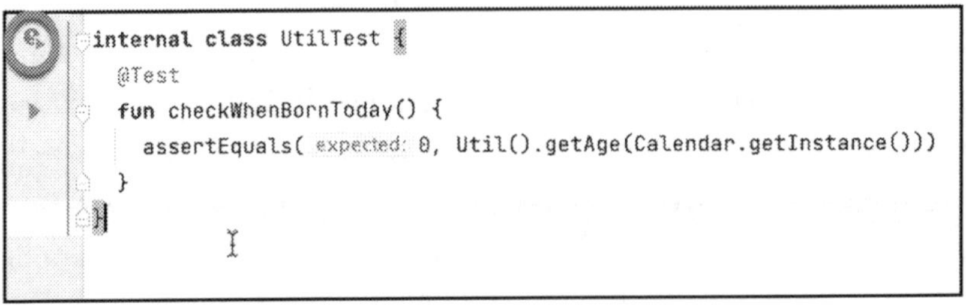

```
internal class UtilTest {
    @Test
    fun checkWhenBornToday() {
        assertEquals( expected: 0, Util().getAge(Calendar.getInstance()))
    }
}
```

Figure 9-10. *Run the test again*

Did you notice the gutter arrow next to checkWhenBornToday() function doesn't have the exclamation icon? It's still just a green arrow; that's because we haven't run a failing test on that function yet.

The test succeeds. Did you notice the green check marks on the tool window (Figure 9-11)? Notice also the gutter arrows on the main editor. When the tests are passing, the icons in the gutter are green dots with a check mark (not red dots with exclamations).

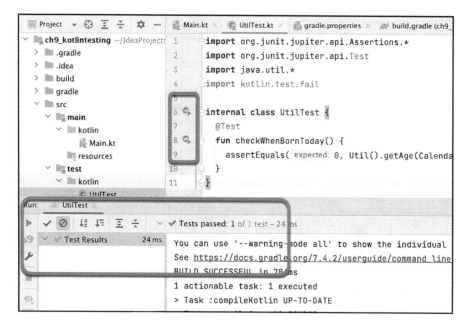

Figure 9-11. *Test succeeds*

The test passed (as expected) because we hardcoded the return value of zero in Util().getAge().

Iterate

Let's add another test. Edit the UtilTest class to match the following code (shown in Listing 9-1).

Listing 9-1. UtilTest, with a new test

```kotlin
internal class UtilTest {
  @Test
  fun checkWhenBornToday() {
    assertEquals(0, Util().getAge(Calendar.getInstance()))
  }
```

```
@Test
fun checkWhenBorn5000DaysAgo() {                    //#1
    val tempdate = Calendar.getInstance()          //#2
    tempdate.add(Calendar.DAY_OF_YEAR, - 5000)     //#3
    assertEquals(13, Util().getAge(tempdate))      //#4
}
```

#1 Let's create a new test and name it checkWhenBorn5000DaysAgo.

#2 Store a Calendar object to tempdate. Initialize it to the current date and time.

#3 Pass a negative five thousand (days) value to the add() function of the Calendar object.

#4 Five thousand days is roughly 13 years, so let's use that on the assert. Save the file, then run the test again.

One test passed (checkWhenBornToday), but one test failed (checkWhenBorn5000DaysAgo), as shown in Figure 9-12. It's expected. The getAge() function still has the hard-coded return value (zero). Let's fix that now.

```
 5
 6  ⬢   internal class UtilTest {
 7          @Test
 8  ⬢       fun checkWhenBornToday() {
 9              assertEquals( expected: 0, Util().getAge(Calendar.getInstance()))
10          }
11
12          @Test
13  ⬢       fun checkWhenBorn5000DaysAgo() {
14              val tempdate : Calendar! = Calendar.getInstance()
15              tempdate.add(Calendar.DAY_OF_YEAR,   amount: - 5000)
16              assertEquals( expected: 13, Util().getAge(tempdate))
17          }
18      }
```

⊗ Tests failed: 1, passed: 1 of 2 tests - 29 ms

```
Starting Gradle Daemon...
Gradle Daemon started in 1 s 738 ms
> Task :wrapper
Deprecated Gradle features were used in this build, making it incompatible
You can use '--warning-mode all' to show the individual deprecation warning
See https://docs.gradle.org/7.4.2/userguide/command line interface.html#sec
```

Figure 9-12. *One passed and one failed test*

Let's edit the getAge() function to behave as intended—an actual age calculator. Listing 9-2 shows the refactored getAge() function.

Listing 9-2. Util.kt

```kotlin
import java.util.*

class Util {

  fun getAge (birthdate: Calendar): Int {
    var today = Calendar.getInstance()
```

```
var age = today.get(Calendar.YEAR) - birthdate.
get(Calendar.YEAR)

return age
  }
}
```

Run the test again.

This time, both are our test passes (shown in Figure 9-13).

```
 6      internal class UtilTest {
 7          @Test
 8          fun checkWhenBornToday() {
 9              assertEquals( expected: 0, Util().getAge(Calendar.getInstance()))
10          }
11
12          @Test
13          fun checkWhenBorn5000DaysAgo() {
14              val tempdate : Calendar! = Calendar.getInstance()
15              tempdate.add(Calendar.DAY_OF_YEAR, amount: - 5000)
16              assertEquals( expected: 13, Util().getAge(tempdate))
17          }
18      }
```

```
✓ Tests passed: 2 of 2 tests - 26 ms

> Task :wrapper
Deprecated Gradle features were used in this build, making it incompatible w
You can use '--warning-mode all' to show the individual deprecation warnings
See https://docs.gradle.org/7.4.2/userguide/command_line_interface.html#sec:
BUILD SUCCESSFUL in 765ms
1 actionable task: 1 executed
```

Figure 9-13.   Both tests passed

You can write more tests for the getAge() function. For example, you can check the return value if you pass a date in the future, or a hundred thousand days ago, etc. The point is to be rigorous and thorough in your testing. For additional reading on how to create tests, might I suggest looking into the topic of "boundary value analysis"; it's a software testing technique where tests are designed to include representatives of boundary values in a range.

Key Takeaways

- Unit tests have narrow scopes; they test something very specific, like "check the age when born today".

- Name the tests descriptively so they become self-documenting within the test code.

- It's okay to start with failing tests. Keep refactoring your codes until all tests are passing.

CHAPTER 10

Writing Idiomatic Kotlin

Kotlin was designed to be very similar to Java to attract the current crop of Java devs. Kotlin's similarity to Java makes the transition smooth and almost frictionless. Kotlin was also designed so that devs can write codes more expressively; to do this, you can't just use Kotlin but still code using Java thought patterns. You need to recognize—and apply as much as possible—the language idioms of Kotlin.

What we'll cover:

- Null checks and safe casts

- Named and default arguments

- Expressions

- apply()

- Extension functions

We already covered these topics in Chapters 2 ("A Quick Tour of Kotlin"), 3 ("Functions"), 4 ("Types"), and 5 ("Higher Order Functions"). This chapter should serve nicely as a refresher.

© Ted Hagos 2023
T. Hagos, *Beginning Kotlin*, https://doi.org/10.1007/978-1-4842-8698-2_10

Null Checks and Safe Casts

Null references are a major source of headaches in Java. While it is possible to do null checks, it's cumbersome, verbose, and easy to miss.

Consider Listing 10-1; you may remember this code from Chapter 8, "Debugging". We're counting the occurrence of every word in a string. To do this, we use a mutable Map to store each word as we encounter it. If the word isn't on the map yet, we create a new entry for the word (becomes the key), and then we put a value of 1. If the word is already on the map, we update the value (increment by 1).

Listing 10-1. WordFrequency.kt

```
var str = "the quick brown fox the quick brown fox
jumped over"

var words = str.split(" ")
var unique: MutableMap<String, Int> =
mutableMapOf<String, Int>()

words.forEach {
  word -> if (unique.containsKey(word)) {
    var temp: Int? = unique[word]          //#1
      if (temp == null) {                  //#2
        throw IllegalStateException()
      }
      else {
        temp = temp + 1                    //#3
      }
    unique[word] = temp
  }
  else {
    unique.put(word, 1)
```

```
    }
  }
println(unique)
```

#1 Can return a null value.

#2 Let's do the null check; if it returns null, we throw an exception.

#3 If it's not null, it's safe to increment.

The above code shows how you would go about the nullability problem using Java thought patterns. You may still do this in Kotlin; it will still compile and run without problems, or you could use Kotlin's language capabilities to decrease verbosity and increase expressiveness like this

```
var temp: Int? = unique[word]
temp = temp?: throw IllegalStateException()
temp = temp + 1
```

The Elvis operator (?:) means that if the expression to its left is not null, return that. If it is null, return the expression to its right. In the preceding code snippet, the expression to the left of Elvis is just *temp* (the variable). So, if *temp* is not null, we simply return the value of *temp*. If *temp* is null, we return what's on the right of Elvis (which is a call to throw an Exception).

Another way to handle the nullability is to use the safe call and double bang operator (!!), like this

```
var temp: Int? = unique[word]
temp = temp?.plus(1)!!
```

The statement `temp = temp + 1` is actually implemented as an operator overload; it translates to `temp.plus(1)`.

The safe call (?.) operator in the preceding code means the increment will happen only if *temp* is not null.

The use of !! (not-null assertion operator) converts any value to a non-null type and throws an exception if the value is null. So, temp?.plus(1)!! means we're converting the whole expression to a non-null value, and in the event that *temp* really is null, the runtime will throw an NPE (NullPointerException).

This topic was discussed in Chapter 2, "A Quick Tour of Kotlin," section "Handling Nulls".

Data Classes

Data classes are one of the more popular features of Kotlin.

Imagine that you have the following class definition (in Java):

```java
class Person {
  String lastName;
  String firstName;

  Person(String fname, String lname) {
    lastName = lname;
    firstName = fname;
  }
}
```

Imagine that we stored instances of the Person class into ArrayLists, then try to compare the ArrayLists, like this

```java
Person jim = new Person("Jim", "Smith");

List arr1 = new ArrayList<Person>();
List arr2 = new ArrayList<Person>();

arr1.add(jim);
arr2.add(jim);

if (arr1 == arr2) {
  System.out.println("arr1 == arr2");
```

```
}
else {
  System.out.println("not equal");
}
```

The program outputs "not equal". Of course. But surely, you can see the intent in the code. If you want the code to work the way we intend, which is to compare the ArrayLists for equivalence like we were comparing primitives, you need to do some work like overriding the Person class' equals(), hashCode(), and toString() methods—which we won't do here—to make them work with Collections the way we intended.

With Kotlin data classes, we can write codes like this

```
data class Person (val firstName:String,
                   val lastName:String) {

}


fun main(args: Array<String>) {
  var arr1 = mutableListOf<Person>()
  var arr2 = mutableListOf<Person>()

  val jim = Person("Jim", "Jones")

  arr1.add(jim)
  arr2.add(jim)

  println("arr1 == arr2 :  ${arr1 == arr2}") // this
just works!
}
```

The equals(), hashCode(), and toString() methods were conveniently taken care of by using data classes. It's a lot less work.

This topic was discussed in Chapter 4, "Types".

Named and Default Arguments

You can define default values for function parameters. This lets you call the function without specifying all (or any) arguments. This effectively lets you define default values for the function parameters; like this

```
fun connectToDb(hostname: String = "localhost",
                username: String = "mysql",
                password:String = "secret") {
}
```

Notice that "localhost", "mysql", and "secret" were assigned to hostname, username, and password, respectively. You can call the function like this

```
connectToDb("mycomputer","root")
```

I didn't pass the third argument in the code snippet above, but that is still a valid call because all of the function's parameters have default values. I can even call the function without passing any argument at all like this

```
connectToDb()
```

With default arguments, you won't need to use method overloads anymore—although you can still do function overloading in Kotlin, you probably have less reason to do it because of default parameters.

Named Parameters

Going back to the preceding code sample, If we call the connectToDb() function and pass all the arguments, the call looks like the following:

```
connectToDb("neptune", jupiter", "saturn")
```

Can you spot the problem? That is a valid call because all parameters of connectToDb() are *Strings*, and we passed three *String* arguments. It isn't clear from the call site which one is the username, the hostname, or the password. In Java, this ambiguity problem is solved by various workarounds, including commenting on the call site like this

```
connectoToDb(/* hostname*/, "neptune,
            /* username*/ "jupiter",
            /*password*/ "saturn")
```

We don't have to do this in Kotlin because we can name the argument at the call site like this

```
connecToDb(hostname = "neptune",
           username = "jupiter",
           password = "saturn")
```

You must remember that when you start to specify the argument name, you need to specify the names of all the following arguments to avoid confusion; besides, Kotlin won't let you compile such codes. For example, if we did something like the following:

```
connectToDb(hostname = "neptune",
            username = "jupiter",
            "saturn")
```

That isn't allowed because once we name the second argument (*username*), we need to provide the name of all the arguments that come after it. And in the example above, the second argument is named but not the third one. On the other hand, a call like the following:

```
connectToDb("neptune",
            username = "jupiter",
            password = "saturn")
```

The preceding call is allowed. It's okay that we didn't name the first argument because Kotlin treats it as a regular call and uses the positional value of the argument to resolve the parameter. Then we named all the remaining arguments.

This topic was discussed in Chapter 3, "Functions".

Expressions

In Java, the *if* is a statement, while in Kotlin, it's an expression—which means it returns a value.

For example, instead of writing this

```
val dow:Int = getDayOfWeek()
var day:String = ""

if (dow == 6) {
  day = "Friday"
}
else {
  day = "Who cares"
}
```

You can write something like this

```
val dow:Int = getDayOfWeek()
var day:String = if (dow == 6) {
  "Friday"
}
else {
  "Who cares"
}
```

This topic was discussed in Chapter 2, "A Quick Tour of Kotlin", section "Controlling Program Flow".

apply()

The apply() function is handy because it lets us do multiple operations on the same object without repeating its name.

Instead of doing this

```
val dbCon = MyDB()
dbCon.hostname = "server201"
dbCon.username = "tghagos"
dbCon.password = "dontaskme"
```

You can simply write this

```
val dbCon = MyDB().apply {
  hostname = "server201"
  username = "tghagos"
  password = "dontaskme"
```

This topic was discussed in Chapter 5, "Higher Order Functions".

Extension Functions

In Java, if we needed to add functionality to a class, we could either add methods to the class itself or extend it by inheritance, then add the new method to the child class. An *extension function* in Kotlin lets us add behavior to an existing class (including ones written in Java) without using inheritance. It lets us define a function that can be invoked as a class member, but the function is implemented outside the class.

Consider the following class:

```
fun main(args: Array<String>) {
  val msg = "My name is Maximus Decimus Meridius"
  println(homerify(msg))
  println(chanthofy(msg))
```

```kotlin
  println(terminatorify(msg))

}


fun homerify(msg: String) = "$msg -- woohoo!"
fun chanthofy(msg: String) = "Chan, $msg , tho"
fun terminatorify(msg: String) = "$msg -- I'll be back"
```

The preceding code has three functions that take a String argument, add some Strings to it and then return them to the caller; it's simple.

We can consolidate the code a bit more by putting all three functions (homerify, chantofy, and terminatorify) in a single class (which becomes our utility class)—shown below:

```kotlin
fun main(args: Array<String>) {
  val msg = "My name is Maximus Decimus Meridius"

  val util = StringUtil()
  println(util.homerify(msg))
  println(util.chanthofy(msg))
  println(util.terminatorify(msg))
}
/*
  The StringUtil class consolidates our three methods as member
  functions.
  This is a very common Java practice.
*/
class StringUtil {
  fun homerify(msg: String) = "$msg -- woohoo!"
  fun chanthofy(msg:String) = "Chan, $msg , tho"
  fun terminatorify(msg: String) = "$msg -- I'll be back"
}
```

The preceding code is a very common practice in Java. It's considered a good idea to consolidate related methods into a utility class. Although Java programmers might have implemented `homerify()`, `chanthofy()`, and `terminatorify()` as static methods and not instance methods like we did here, but that's okay. The point is, in Kotlin, instead of writing a utility class for the three methods, we can rewrite our methods in a much simpler way. We can simply write this

```
fun String.homerify() = "$this -- woohoo!"
```

The code snippet above looks deceptively simple, but this is really all it takes to write an extension function.

Extension functions introduce the concept of a *receiver* type and a *receiver* object. In our example, the *receiver* type is *String*—it's the class to which we'd like to add our extension function. The *receiver* object is the instance of that type, which in our example is *"My name is Maximus Decimus Meridius"*. When you attach an extension function to a type, such as a *String,* in our case, the extension function can reference the receiver object using the keyword *this.*

An extension function appears just like any member function defined on the *receiver* type. So, it makes sense for the extension function to be able to reference *this.* Here's the code for our extended String class:

```
fun main(args: Array<String>) {
  val msg = "My name is Maximus Decimus Meridius"

  println(msg.homerify())
  println(msg.chanthofy())
  println(msg.terminatorify())

}

fun String.homerify() = "$this -- woohoo!"
fun String.chanthofy() = "Chan, $this , tho"
fun String.terminatorify() = "$this -- I'll be back"
```

You can still write utility functions in Kotlin. Still, with extension functions at our disposal, it seems more natural to use them because it increases the semantic value of the code. It feels more natural to use extension function syntax.

This topic was discussed in Chapter 3, "Functions", section "Extension Functions".

Key Takeaways

- Before you write a utility class in Kotlin, consider first if your needs can be served (quicker) by an extension function.

- If, when, try, and do are expressions in Kotlin. They're not statements. They can return values. Your codes might be more succinct if you use these constructs as expressions.

- If you're writing POJOs, use data classes; the equals(), hashCode(), toString() (and even the copy()) methods are automatically—and properly—implemented for you. You don't need to bother with boiler-plate

CHAPTER 11

Creating a Spring Boot Project

Building an application is hard work. There are a ton of decisions to make, and plenty of things can go wrong. Using software frameworks relieves some of these headaches.

Spring is probably one of the most—if not the most—popular framework for the JVM. The Spring framework is a game changer for Java development. Now, you can build Spring apps with Kotlin too.

What we'll cover:

- Spring and Spring Boot

- How to bootstrap a Spring Boot project using the Initializr

Spring and Spring Boot

The Spring framework is built and designed such that it provides comprehensive support for developing applications for the JVM, including abstractions for some of the most powerful and common enterprise systems integrations, specifically around common infrastructure.

Spring is designed to provide plumbing for using enterprise offerings and common components used in application development. These plumbings let you take advantage of enterprise offerings without getting

© Ted Hagos 2023
T. Hagos, *Beginning Kotlin*, https://doi.org/10.1007/978-1-4842-8698-2_11

bogged down in boiler-plate code; Spring. Lets you focus on your business logic.

Before Spring came about, we used JEE (Java Enterprise Edition)—J2EE, actually; but J2EE was difficult to use and heavy. It taxed both computing resources and developer patience. Then Rod Johnson introduced Spring. It's a lightweight framework as it tries to be as invisible as possible, which is achieved by using POJO (Plain Old Java Object) instead of Enterprise Java Beans (EJB).

The Spring Family

When people say Spring, it can actually mean a number of things; it could mean the framework, Spring Boot, Spring Cloud, Spring Batch, Spring Security, etc. Most often, "Spring" refers to Spring's entire family of projects.

Spring started with the Spring framework. This is what started it all. It was a response to the complexity of building apps using (then) heavyweight J2EE—now called JEE, and so much better and improved. Spring framework aimed to remove the complexity and make web development and data access easier for developers.

The success of Spring framework led to the creation of other Spring projects, which are still based on the Spring framework but tailored to specific domains. For example,

- Spring Security

- Spring for Apache Kafka

- Spring Cloud

- Spring Batch

- Spring Social

- Spring Data

- Spring Integration

- Spring Boot

- Etc.

Spring Boot is one of the Spring projects that made a big impact on software development. While Spring already simplified enterprise development (as compared to a J2EE project), there were still a couple of things to deal with, like choice-making, configuration, and a cumbersome deployment model. Spring Boot changed that by taking an opinionated view of building Spring-based applications. Using Spring Boot means accepting some defaults for lots of things, for example, library choices, configuration, and auto-detecting configurations. Spring Boot also revolutionized the deployment model; you could run a Spring-based app without deploying it to a web container like Tomcat (for example). You could run a web app by simply running a jar file.

Spring Initializr

There are a couple of ways to bootstrap a Spring Boot project. You can either use the Spring Boot CLI (command line interface) or the Spring Initializr, or you can create it manually (I don't recommend this) to create a Spring project.

A popular way of bootstrapping a Spring project is to use the Spring Initializr. Launch the browser and go to https://start.spring.io/. You should see the initializer (Figure 11-1).

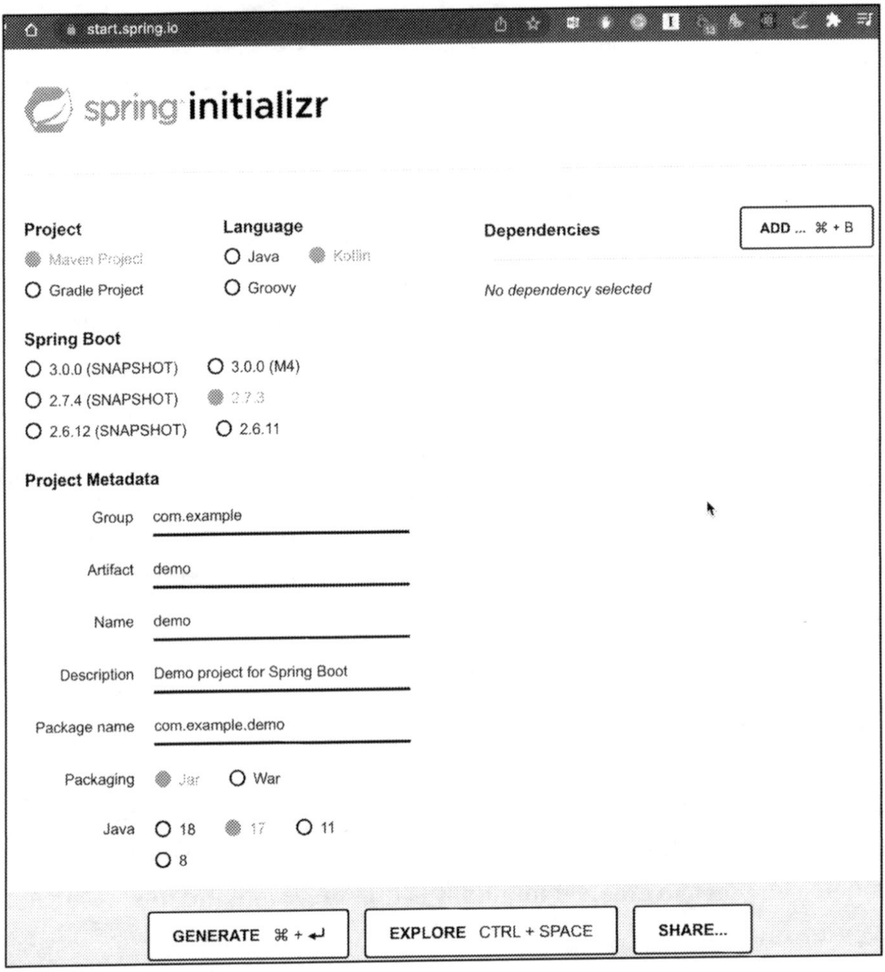

Figure 11-1. Spring Initializr

You can choose whether to use Maven or Gradle for the build tool (I chose Maven). You can choose which version of Spring Boot to use (I went with the default, which is 2.7.3). You can name the project, the package name, and artifact name—I went for all the defaults. I didn't change anything. Also, don't forget to select Kotlin as the language.

Choose the packaging (whether jar or war). Choose the Java version as well (I went with Java 17).

The next thing to do is to choose the dependencies. Click the **ADD** button. Type the name of the dependency on the search bar, then click to choose it (see Figure 11-2).

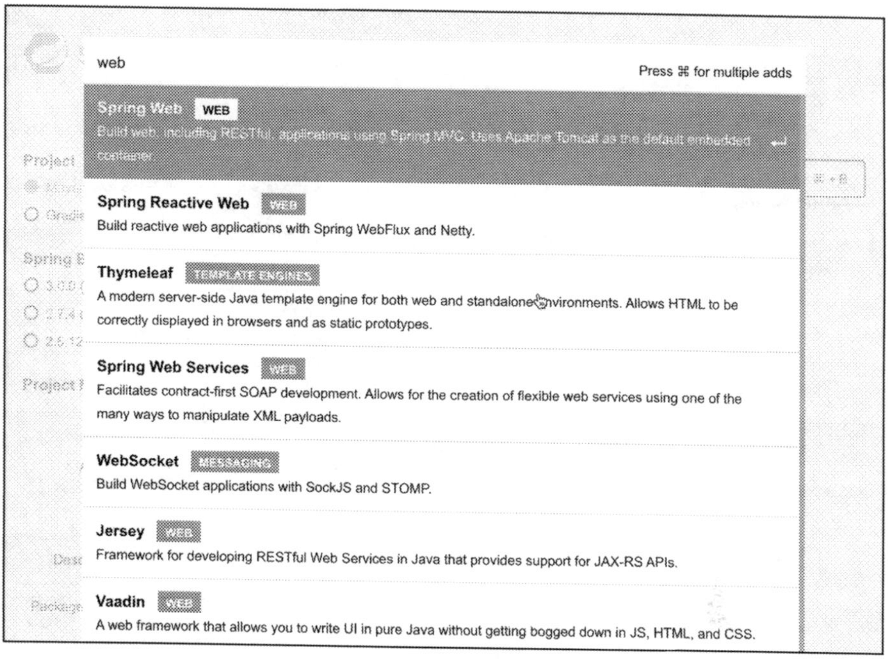

Figure 11-2. *Add dependencies*

Repeat the process until all your dependencies are added. Once done, click the **GENERATE** button (seen in Figure 11-3).

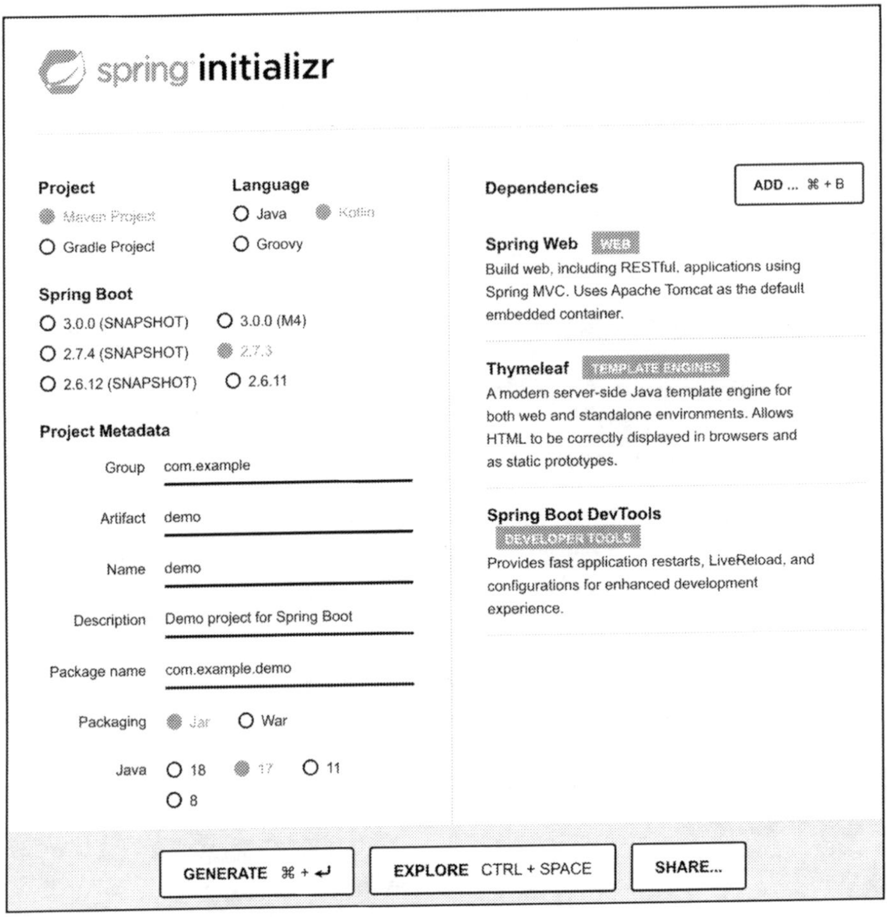

Figure 11-3. Dependencies added

The generated project will be downloaded to your machine. The downloaded zipped file is named *demo.zip* (in my case) because the project is named demo (see Figure 11-3). The zipped file takes the name of the project.

Unzip the project file, then put the project file where you usually store IntelliJ projects. In my case, this is ~/IdeaProjects.

In IntelliJ, use the main menu bar **File ➤ New ➤ Project from Existing Sources** (Figure 11-4).

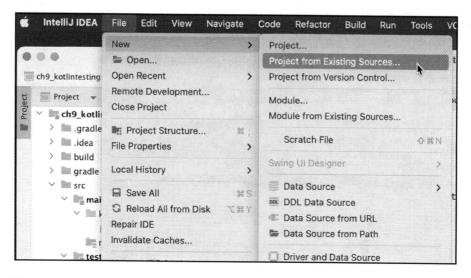

Figure 11-4. *Open project from Existing sources*

In the file explorer or Finder window, select the name of the generated Spring Boot project (Figure 11-5).

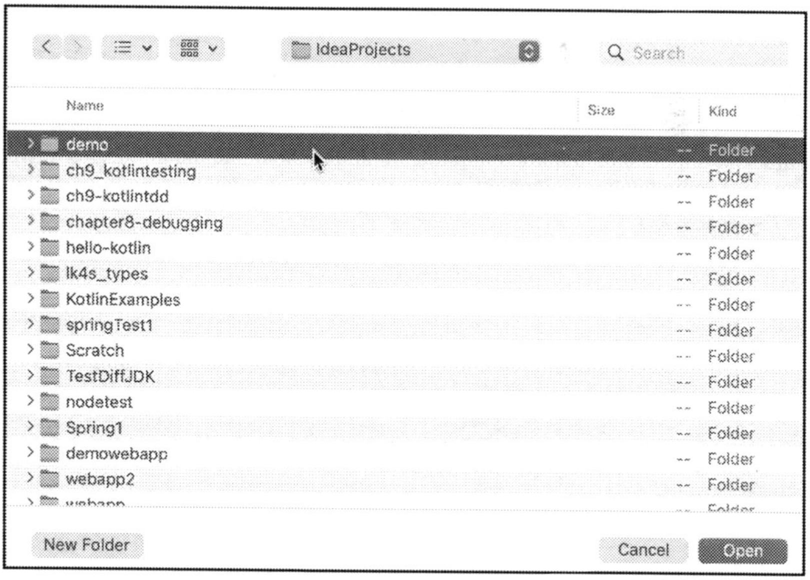

Figure 11-5. *Find the generated project*

Click **Open** to proceed.

In the screen that follows, choose "Import project from an external model", making sure that Maven is selected (Figure 11-6).

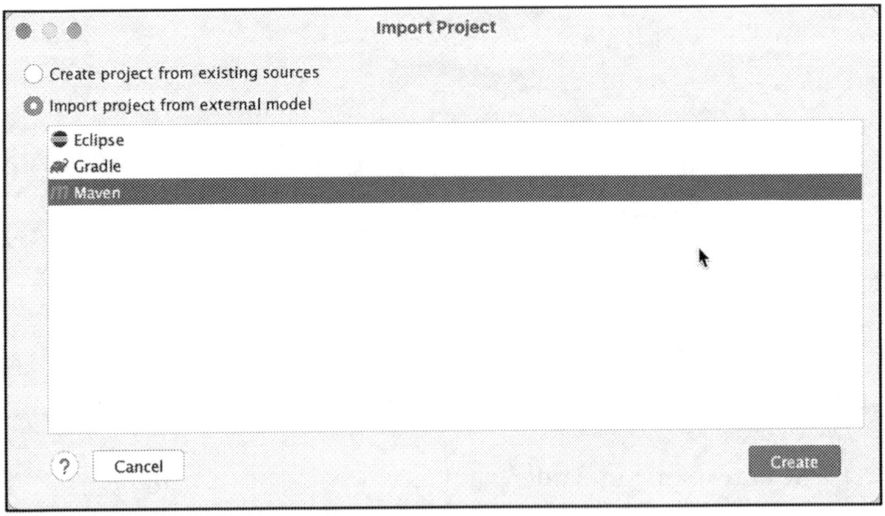

Figure 11-6. *Import project*

Click **Create** to proceed. IntelliJ will pull all dependencies and necessary libraries.

Figure 11-7 shows the demo project after we've imported it into IntelliJ.

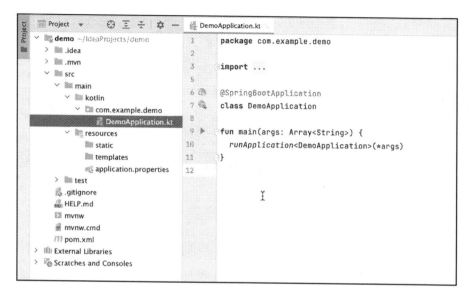

Figure 11-7. *Demo project*

Listing 11-1 shows the generated DemoApplication.kt file.

Listing 11-1. DemoApplication.kt

```
package com.example.demo

import org.springframework.boot.autoconfigure.
SpringBootApplication
import org.springframework.boot.runApplication

@SpringBootApplication
class DemoApplication                              //#1

fun main(args: Array<String>) {                    //#2
 runApplication<DemoApplication>(*args)
}
```

#1 We don't have to declare the class as open; the Kotlin-spring plugin will do that for us.

#2 In Java, Spring Boot looks for public static void main(String [ ]args) as the entry point. In Kotlin, it's okay to write the entry point as a top-level function.

Let's create an endpoint. Edit DemoApplication.kt to match Listing 11-2.

Listing 11-2. DemoApplication.kt, with endpoints

```kotlin
package com.example.demo

import org.springframework.boot.autoconfigure.
SpringBootApplication
import org.springframework.boot.runApplication
import org.springframework.web.bind.annotation.GetMapping
import org.springframework.web.bind.annotation.RestController

@SpringBootApplication
class DemoApplication

fun main(args: Array<String>) {
 runApplication<DemoApplication>(*args)
}
data class Message(val id:String?,  val text: String)

@RestController
class MessageResource {
 @GetMapping
 fun index(): List<Message> = listOf(
  Message("1", "Hello!"),
  Message("2", "Hola!"),
  Message("3", "Kon'nichiwa"),
 )
}
```

Start the app. You can use the arrow on the gutter next to `fun main()`, as shown in Figure 11-8.

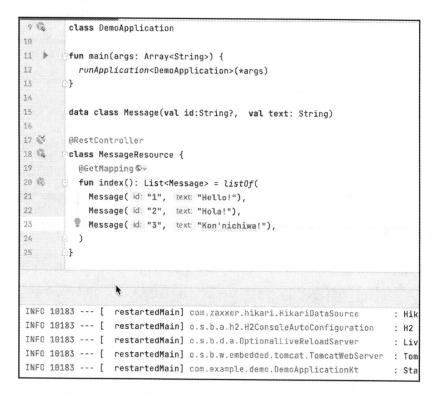

```
 9     class DemoApplication
10
11  ▶  fun main(args: Array<String>) {
12         runApplication<DemoApplication>(*args)
13     }
14
15     data class Message(val id:String?,  val text: String)
16
17     @RestController
18     class MessageResource {
19       @GetMapping
20       fun index(): List<Message> = listOf(
21         Message( id: "1",  text: "Hello!"),
22         Message( id: "2",  text: "Hola!"),
23         Message( id: "3",  text: "Kon'nichiwa!"),
24       )
25     }
```

```
INFO 10183 --- [  restartedMain] com.zaxxer.hikari.HikariDataSource          : Hik
INFO 10183 --- [  restartedMain] o.s.b.a.h2.H2ConsoleAutoConfiguration       : H2
INFO 10183 --- [  restartedMain] o.s.b.d.a.OptionalLiveReloadServer          : Liv
INFO 10183 --- [  restartedMain] o.s.b.w.embedded.tomcat.TomcatWebServer     : Tom
INFO 10183 --- [  restartedMain] com.example.demo.DemoApplicationKt          : Sta
```

Figure 11-8. *DemoApplication, started*

To see the results, launch a browser and go to `http://localhost:8080`

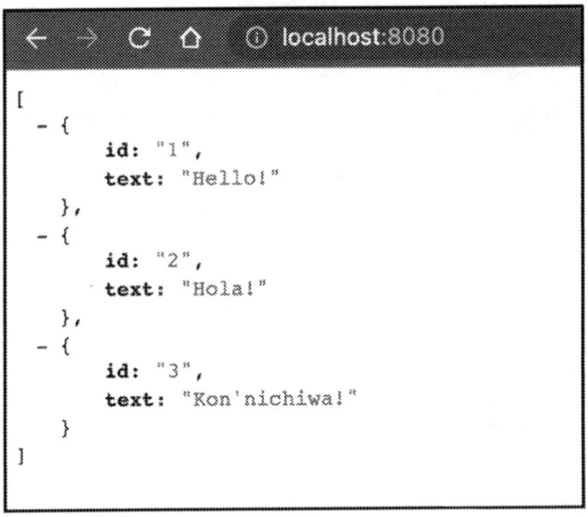

Figure 11-9. DemoApplication.kt, running

Key Takeaways

- Starting a project can be difficult, confusing, and frustrating because of the myriad things you need to do. It can sometimes be hard to see where to begin. Spring Boot can ease that if you're willing to follow its world-view.

- The Spring Initializr is the simplest way to bootstrap a Spring project.

Index

A

answer() function, 78
apply() function, 119, 121, 122, 209
arrayOf() function, 39, 125
arrayOfNulls function, 39, 124, 125
Arrays, 38, 39
    Kotlin, 124
assertEquals(), 193

B

Basic types
    arrays, 38, 39
    Booleans, 37
    characters, 36, 37
    numbers/literal constants, 34–36
    strings/strings templates, 39–42
bigSmall() function, 60
Blocks, 23, 31, 32, 44, 49, 52, 85, 163, 164, 170, 172
Booleans, 22, 34, 37, 43, 148
Built-in functions, 38, 119, 140

C

Characters, 36, 37
checkWhenBornToday() function, 193, 194, 196

Classes
    basic class, 83
    creating objects, 84
    data objects
        collection objects, 99
        compare objects, 99
        comparison, 99
        Employee data class, 101, 102
        equals() function, 99–101
        hashCode() function, 100, 101
    new keyword, 84
Closures, 118, 119, 122
Collections
    definition, 123
    framework, 128, 129
    interfaces, 129
    Kotlin, 128, 140
    library functions, 130
    lists, 130–132
    maps, 133–135
    sets, 132, 133
    traversal, 136, 137
Collections framework, 123, 128, 129, 134, 135, 140
Command line interface (CLI), 215

© Ted Hagos 2023
T. Hagos, *Beginning Kotlin*, https://doi.org/10.1007/978-1-4842-8698-2

Printed in the United States
by Baker & Taylor Publisher Services